ABI GEZUNT!

CLASSIC JOKES FROM THE JEWISH PRESS

Two Lights
PUBLISHING צוי ליכט

WRITTEN BY ARNOLD FINE

COMPILED BY ZALMAN GOLDSTEIN

DEDICATED TO

Avraham (Arnold) Fine

Beloved JEWISH PRESS Columnist
and Senior Editor

Abi Gezunt!
Classic Jokes from The Jewish Press

Written by Arnold Fine
Compiled by Zalman Goldstein

FIRST PRINTING

Reprinted with permission from
The Jewish Press and the Klass family

An imprint of
The Jewish Learning Group, Inc.
Tel. 1-888-565-3276
www.JewishLearningGroup.com

Comments, Information and Orders
Info@AbiGezuntJokes.com

ISBN-13: 978-1-891293-02-3

INQUIRE ABOUT OUR
BULK AND INSTITUTIONAL DISCOUNTS

Table of Laughs

Introduction

Everyone who knew Arnold Fine describes him as a kind, wise and warm-hearted person. Those who worked with him for decades also describe Arnie, as he was affectionately called, as super-talented and enormously dedicated to his work. Above all, his keen sense of humor was the one thing about which everyone raved.

Born in the Bronx in 1924, Fine grew up experiencing the sights, sounds and smells of New York City in the 1930's and 1940's, which contributed greatly to his later writings. After joining the Navy at the end of WWII, and, a few weeks later, finding himself drafted into the Army, he had the distinction of serving in both the Navy and the Army.

Following the war, Fine worked as a press photographer for several newspapers. Earning his bachelor's degree via the GI bill and later on, adding a masters in education, led him to become a celebrated Special-Ed teacher in the New York

City school system where he pioneered in teaching children with special needs.

In the late 1950's, while shopping his photography services to local newspapers, he met **Rabbi Shalom Klass**, then publisher of the **Brooklyn Weekly** and the one who would later go on to found **The Jewish Press**. The rest, as they say, is history.

Avraham (Arnold) Fine (1924-2014)

Fine's warm and friendly writing style spoke to generations of readers both Jewish and non-Jewish alike, and helped build the fledgling **Jewish Press** weekly into one of America's top Jewish newspapers.

A music lover, who also played clarinet, saxophone and piano, Fine's creativity never seemed to end. He would teach in the morning and work at **The Jewish Press** for the rest of the day. He started out with writing the paper's front-page stories and other news articles. Given his knack for words and human emotions, he quickly expanded into other editorial functions.

As his formidable command of the English language became evident, he was promoted to editor of the paper and eventually senior editor, a post he held proudly and successfully for many decades.

In addition to his serious journalistic writings, Fine's humorous nature found expression in several delightful and light-hearted serial columns which he lovingly tended and nurtured throughout the years, drawing him a fiercely loyal readership. These included the well-loved feature *"The Silly World of Chelm,"* which offered side-splitting tales from the legendary town of Chelm, and *"I Remember When!,"* a charmingly written and highly-entertaining column recalling his memories of growing up in New York City.

One of his most memorable gems was the joke-of-the-week feature which tenaciously appeared at the bottom corner of the last page, under the heading *"Abi Gezunt!"* (Yiddish for, "At least we are healthy!"). Generous by nature, Fine wouldn't let a week go by without sharing a funny joke or story that he recently heard or made up. For many, the humorous yarns and witticisms that he dispensed was their first stop before tackling the week's headlines.

Fine retired at the age of eighty, after more than fifty years of dedicated service at *The Jewish Press.* He later developed Parkinson's disease and several years later, in 2014, passed away in his sleep. He was buried at the New Montefiore Jewish Cemetery in West Babylon, New York.

Fine was predeceased by his wife, in 2006, and is survived by three children, many grandchildren and great-grandchildren. May his good name and good memory be a blessing!

☆☆

A natural follow up to our recently published book, *"The Silly World of Chelm"* — which gathered more than one hundred and fifty Chelm tales from the pages of *The Jewish Press* — was bringing together nearly half-a-century of *"Abi Gezunt!"* material for everyone's continued delight. The results, following months of laborious yet very enjoyable effort span two charming volumes.

The present volume contains material relating to *City Life, Jewish Wit, Politics and High Office, Israel, Doctors and Medicine, Old Age, Relationships* and *Little Gems.*

Volume two wraps up with *Money and Business, Law and Order, Food and Dining, Parenting and Children, Education, The Pulpit* and *Travel.*

Eternal thanks to *Arnold Fine* for making us laugh so often and for training us to see and enjoy the lighter side of life.

Tremendous thanks to *Naomi Mauer* and the entire *Klass Family,* for permitting me, once again, to mine, edit, and reprint everyone's beloved material from *The Jewish Press.*

And, once more, huge thanks to *Jerry Greenwald* and *Chumi Friedman,* for their ready assistance with navigating the mountainous archives of *The Jewish Press.*

Last, but not least, special thanks to *Heshy Kornblit,* for getting the ball rolling from the start, *Ginny Westcott* and *Aryeh Friedman* for creative input, and *Hershel Rosenbluh* and *my children* for proofreading.

Abi Gezunt!

Zalman Goldstein
Zalman@ZalmanGoldstein.com

City Life

. . . .

A buyer of a new, multi-million dollar yacht liked to invite potential clients to his boat for a cruise. In order to make sure nobody would ever turn down his invitation, he would say, "You'll love my new boat! You must come out to see it. As a matter of fact, I named it after you!"

No one could resist the pitch. It was only after they came down to the boat that they realized that they had been had. The letters printed on the stern of the boat read, "AFTER YOU!"

. . . .

A cab driver was overheard complaining to a passenger, "This 50 cent tip is an insult!"

"Oh?" the passenger said. "How much should it be?"

"Another 50 cents, at least!" said the Cabbie.

"My dear man," replied the passenger, "I wouldn't dream of insulting you twice!"

. . . .

A fancy lady was showing some friends around New York city. A panhandler walked up to her and said, "Lady, could you spare a quarter for a cup of coffee?"

The lady turned indignantly and snapped, "I don't give money to people on the street!"

The beggar turned innocently and replied, "Lady, what should I do? Open an office?"

. . . .

A fellow had just picked up an old Grandfather Clock at an auction. As he was carrying it down the street, unable to see where he was going, he bumped into a drunk.

The drunk, knocked to the ground, staggered to his feet and snapped, "What's the matter with you, buddy? Can't you wear a wrist-watch like everybody else?"

. . . .

A fellow is driving down the street with a car full of penguins and stopped at a red light. A police officer walked over to the car and exclaimed, "Hey, what are you doing? You can't drive around with a car full of penguins. You better take them to the zoo!" The fellow nodded and drove off.

The following day, the fellow stopped for the light at the same street corner.

"Hey, are you a wise guy?" shouted the cop. "I told you yesterday to take the penguins to the zoo!"

The fellow nodded, "I did! We had such a good time that today I'm taking them roller-skating!"

. . . .

A fellow was arguing with a welfare recipient. "Let me ask you something," he began. "Why don't you go to school, get an education and get a decent job? Then you can save your money, invest it in some blue-chip securities and you'll become rich and never have to work again."

The loafer shrugged his shoulders aimlessly and explained, "Why go through all that when I don't have to work now?"

. . . .

A friend of mine has finally developed a foolproof system for keeping relatives from dropping in on him when he spends weekends at his fancy beach resort dwelling. He told me his trick.

"When the rich ones come," he said, "I borrow money from them. When the poor ones come, I lend them the money — none of them ever come back!"

A Garment Center manufacturer was so incensed with a delinquent customer that he sat down and wrote a scathing note:

"Dear Sir, Who promised to settle up for everything by the first of the month? You! Who failed to keep his promise? You! Who then is a liar? Yours truly, Sam Rabinowitz."

. . . .

A gorilla walked into a neighborhood candy store and ordered an egg-cream. The counterman was a little surprised but he made the drink and served it.

The gorilla handed him a $5 bill and the counterman took it to the back of the store. There he showed it to the boss and said, "Look, a gorilla just ordered an egg cream and gave me a $5 bill. What should I do?"

The boss smiled and said, "Give him a quarter change. I don't think he'll know the difference."

The counterman walked back and handed the gorilla a quarter. The gorilla put the quarter in his pocket and sipped his soda thoughtfully.

The counterman, noticing that the gorilla seemed friendly enough, struck up a conversation and remarked, "You know, we hardly ever get a gorilla in here!"

The gorilla finished his soda and exclaimed, "No wonder! Charging $4.75 for an egg-cream! How many gorillas can afford that?"

A hooligan waving a weapon on a bus in Brooklyn shouted, "Okay, everybody give me your money!" Waving his weapon menacingly, he went from passenger to passenger, taking their money.

Finally, he stopped in front of Goldberg, who reached into his pocket and took out $200 in single bills. Just as the hood began to reach for the money, Goldberg pulled back four dollars from the role of singles.

"Are you out of your mind?" the hood shouted.

Goldberg looked at him indignantly and snapped, "Listen, on a cash transaction like this, I always take my two percent!"

• •

A lady walked into a butcher shop and told the butcher, "Listen, I want a dozen lamb chops — and please make them lean!"

The butcher smiled courteously and replied, "Absolutely! Which way? To the left or to the right?"

• •

A local newspaper accidentally put the name of a very much alive, but not very well liked businessman in their obituary column. No sooner did the paper reach the street when the very irate businessman phoned the editor.

"Sir!" he shouted. "Do you realize that you put my name in the obituary column of today's newspaper?"

The editor hesitated for a moment, then replied slowly, "Yes sir! Where are you calling from now?"

. . . .

A mailman rings the bell of a Brooklyn family. "Excuse me, sir," he said, "Is this package for you? The name is obliterated."

The man smiled and replied, "Nope, that can't be mine. Our name is Oblinsky."

. . . .

A man is waiting in a garage for his car and he's watching a mechanic work on another car. The mechanic changes the oil without spilling a drop. He lifts the hood ever so gently and checks the water level. He lowers the hood very carefully and locks it.

He then cleans the windshield and wipes off all the greasy finger marks on the hood, checks the battery, and, after washing his hands, drives the car slowly into the parking area, leaving plenty of room on each side of the car to make sure another car's door won't hit it.

The man watching all this turns to the shop foreman and says, "Now there's a real mechanic! Look how careful he is with that car."

The foreman replies, "Of course! It's his car!"

A stranger ran up to Shloimy and breathlessly asked, "Have you ever seen a police officer around here?"

Shloimy sighed. "No, there are never any cops around here."

The stranger smiled and said, "Great! Hand me your wallet, this is a stickup!"

. . . .

A man was driving down a country road when he spotted a farmer standing in the middle of a huge field of grass. He pulled his car over to the side of the road and noticed that the farmer was just standing there, doing nothing, looking at nothing.

The man got out of the car, walked all the way to the farmer and asked him, "Ah, excuse me mister, what are you doing?"

"I am trying to win a Nobel Prize." the farmer replied.

"How?" asked the man, puzzled.

"Well, I heard they give the Nobel Prize to people who are out standing in their field."

. . . .

A Martian spaceship landed in the heart of Brooklyn. Suddenly, the door of the spaceship opened and out walked a tiny little Martian. He had on a silver suit, red shoes, red mittens, a red antenna and a little red hat. An old rabbi was passing by and saw this strange phenomenon. He walked up to the little Martian and looked at him strangely.

"Excuse me," the rabbi said softly, "Who are you?"

The Martian said, "I am a Martian!"

The rabbi looked at him curiously, and, noticing the red shoes, asked, "Do all Martians wear red shoes?"

The Martian said, "Yes!"

The rabbi looked at the Martian's gloves and asked, "Do all Martians wear red gloves?"

The Martian replied, "Yes!"

Looking at the Martian's antenna, the rabbi asked, "Do all Martians have red antennas?"

The Martian said, "Yes!"

Noticing the little hat the Martian was wearing, the rabbi asked, "Do all Martians wear red hats?"

The Martian replied, "No, the *goyim* don't."

· ·

A neighbor of mine recently bought a new car and invited me out for a ride. The temperature that day must have been in the 90's, yet he kept every window in the car tightly shut. "Are you crazy?" I questioned. "Why can't we open the windows?"

"Wait a few seconds," my friend said softly, "Wait until we get out of Woodmere. I don't want anybody here to know I didn't get air conditioning."

A non-Jew went with a friend to a Jewish country club to play golf. As they played, the non-Jew said to his friend, "Sol, this place is fabulous. I'd like to join."

"I'm sorry, John," Sol replied. "You have to be Jewish to join this club. You see, the non-Jewish clubs don't let our people join, so that's the way it is here, too."

"Look, I have to join this club. I've never played on such a magnificent golf course!"

Sol replied, "Well, if you really want to join, go to the front desk and tell them your name is Moscowitz, that you're in the Garment Center, and that you manufacture *talleisim*."

John went to the front desk and filled out the application. The president of the club greeted him and said, "I see you manufacture *talleisim*. I always wondered what the writing at the top of the *tallis* says. Can you tell me?"

John sighed and replied, "I really don't know. You see, I just make the sleeves."

. . . .

A not-too-famous local speaker was addressing a Sisterhood meeting. At the end of the talk, the president of the organization stepped forward and handed the speaker a check.

"Oh please," objected the speaker, "I don't want anything for my talk. I would prefer that you use that money for some worthwhile purpose."

"Would you mind if we used it for our special fund?" asked the president of the group.

"Not at all!" exclaimed the speaker. "What is that fund for?"

"To enable us to get a better speaker next year," she replied.

. . . .

A panhandler stopped a lady on the street and said softly, "Ma'am, I haven't eaten in three days!"

With typical Jewish-mother insight, she sighed, "Force yourself!"

. . . .

A rabbi brought his *tallis* into a dry-cleaners to be cleaned. "Mr. Goldberg, how much will you charge me to clean my *tallis*?" the rabbi asked. The dry cleaner smiled and said, "For you rabbi, three dollars."

A few days later, the rabbi returned to the dry cleaner and was confronted by a Chinese gentleman.

"Where's Mr. Goldberg?" the rabbi asked.

"He retired and I bought the store from him."

"Okay," exclaimed the rabbi, "Is my *tallis* ready?"

"Oh, yes," replied the Chinese owner. "That will be $11, please."

"Eleven dollars?" asked the rabbi. "Mr. Goldberg told me it would only be three dollars!"

"I know," replied the Chinese gentleman, "I, too, am charging you three dollars for the cleaning, but I have to charge you $8 more for taking out all the knots in the fringes!"

A rather hefty lady was walking down the street and was stopped by a beggar. "Lady, please," the panhandler said, "I haven't eaten in three days!"

The lady stopped and said, "G-d bless you! I wish I had such willpower!"

. . . .

A rather young Jew applied for a job at a lumber camp in the northwest. "And what do you think you can do?" questioned the burly Irish foreman.

"I'm a lumberjack," the youth answered softly.

"You a lumberjack!" laughed the foreman. "Why, you couldn't even lift an axe. Here, let me see you chop down this little sapling."

The youth picked up the axe, gave one chop, and the sapling fell right to the ground.

"Alright," snapped the foreman, "Let's see you try your hand at this one!" The foreman then pointed to a huge tree.

The youth picked up the axe and walked up to a huge old tree. He took one swing, and sure enough, the tree fell to the ground with the first blow.

"Say," remarked the foreman, "That's fantastic! Normally, it would take two men half a day to knock that tree down. Where did you learn your trade?"

The youth smiled and declared, "In Israel!"

"In Israel?" exclaimed the boss, "Where did you work?"

"In the Sahara Forest," he answered.

"The Sahara Forest?" questioned the boss, "You mean the Sahara desert, don't you!"

The youth smiled and quipped, "No. *Now* it's a desert!"

. . . .

A reporter once asked the Mayor, "How many people work at City Hall?"

The Mayor replied, "About half."

. . . .

A fundraiser went to the office of a wealthy man and asked for a donation. The wealthy man smiled, put his arm around the fundraiser and said, "I've never said no to anyone — go next door and see my assistant."

The fundraiser went next door and spoke with the assistant. She smiled pleasantly and said, "You step next door and speak to the bookkeeper; we've never said no to anyone."

The fundraiser went next door to the bookkeeper, who listened sympathetically. He rose from his desk and said, "You poor dear man, step next door and everything will be taken care of. We've never said no to anybody!"

The fundraiser opened the door and walked into what he thought was another office, but he found himself out in the street.

Just at that moment, he met a friend. "Oh Chaim," the friend exclaimed, "I see you just left the offices of a wealthy man. Did he give you a donation?"

The fundraiser sighed, "No he didn't — but boy, has he got a system!"

. . . .

A teacher was taking a group of youngsters to the Museum of Natural History and everyone was marveling at a huge old oak tree.

The teacher asked the guard, "Can you tell us how old this tree is?"

The guard replied, "Of course! It is estimated to be two-thousand, two-hundred and twenty years, plus fifty-six days old."

"That's amazing!" the teacher exclaimed. "How do you know its age so precisely?"

The guard replied, "Well, when I started working here, they said the tree was estimated to be two-thousand, two-hundred and ten years old, and that was ten years and fifty-six days ago..."

. . . .

A traveling salesman passing through a small Texas town gets off the train and sees a little old man in a rocking chair on the porch of a house. So he stops and says to the little old man, "You don't look as if you have a care in the world. What's your formula for a long and happy life?"

The old man says, "Well, sir, I smoke six packs of cigarettes a day, I drink a quart of bourbon every four hours, and six

cases of beer a week. I never wash, and I don't get to bed until 4:00am"

And the guy says, "Wow, that's just great. How old are you?"

And the little man says, "I'm twenty-two."

. . . .

A truck driver was driving along on the freeway. A sign came up that read, 'Low Bridge Ahead.' Before he knew it, the bridge was right ahead of him and he got stuck under the bridge. Cars were backed up for miles.

Finally, a police car drove up. The cop got out of his car and walked around to the truck driver, put his hands on his hips and said, "Got stuck, huh?"

The truck driver replied, "No. I was delivering this bridge and just ran out of gas!"

. . . .

A wealthy old timer passed away and a short time later, the family gathered for the reading of the will.

"To my wife, I leave all my money and my house," the lawyer solemnly read. "To my sons and daughters, I leave the new cars and all of my books."

"And to my brother-in-law, who always kept saying, 'Health is better than wealth,' I leave my sunlamp."

A young accountant, who was looking for a job, spotted a help wanted ad that looked very promising. The job was said to have short hours, good pay, vacation benefits and more.

The young man answered the ad and went to see the office manager. The office manager was very clever but told the young man that the firm did not want any Jews.

"Aren't you Jewish?" the office manager asked the young accountant. The young man, with obvious Semitic features, cleared his throat and said, "No sir, I'm Turkish. We Turks look a lot like Jews." The office manager seemed pleased and took the young man in to see the boss.

"You look Jewish…" the boss exclaimed.

"He's Turkish, sir," replied the office manager confidently to reassure him that he was not hiring a Jew.

"Okay, that's fine, we have another Turkish fellow in the bookkeeping department," the boss exclaimed. "Get him in here, I'd like to hear you two carry on a conversation in Turkish."

The young man began to get a little nervous. He didn't know what to do. In a few minutes, John the Turk was at the door.

Casting caution to the wind, and not knowing a single word in Turkish, the young man stepped forward, grabbed John the Turk's hand, and said, "*Sholom Aleichem!*"

To his amazement, John the Turk clutched his hand and replied, "*Aleichem Sholom!*"

Now assured that John the Turk was also a Jew, he

continued the conversation, "*Zull der boss shtinken foon kup.*" (The boss's head should go putrid...).

John the Turk replied, "*Gevis!*" (Certainly!)

At this point the boss drew himself up and snapped vehemently, "*Ich hob aich baider in dererd!* (I'm onto both of you...). You're both fired!"

. . . .

A young boy was riding the subway when a little old lady got on the train and stood in front of him in the crowded car. Trained in good manners, the boy started to rise to give his seat to the old woman. However, she pushed him back into his seat and said warmly, "That's not necessary."

The boy smiled back as the train continued on. At the next stop the crowded car became even more crowded, and the boy got up once more, but the old woman gently pushed him back into his seat, repeating, "That's not necessary. I can stand like everyone else."

At the next station the train became even more crowded, and the boy rose once more. And once more, he was pushed back into his seat.

Finally, he shouted, "Lady, lady, please...I'm just trying to get off...I'm already three stops past my station!"

A young fellow was applying for a job. The boss said, "If you can answer these two questions, you got the job." The young man listened.

"How many days in the week begin with the letter 'T'?"

The young man thought for a few minutes, then said, "Two!"

The boss asked, "How did you come up with two?"

The youth smiled and said, "Well, there's 'Today' and 'Tomorrow!'"

The boss scratched his head, then said, "Well, okay. Now tell me, how many seconds are there in a year? Here's a calculator. Figure it out then come back and tell me." The young man took the calculator and went into another room.

Two minutes later, he came out.

"Twelve!" he declared, excitedly.

The man asked, "How did you come up with twelve?"

The youth took a deep breath and said, "There's January 2nd, February 2nd, March 2nd, April 2nd, May 2nd, June 2nd, July 2nd, August 2nd, September 2nd, October 2nd, November 2nd and December 2nd. Like I said, there are twelve seconds in a year!"

So, let me ask you, did he get the job?

. . . .

A young fellow who was anxious to catch his train saw a farmer standing near the edge of the road.

"Excuse me, sir," the young fellow exclaimed. "Would you

mind if I take a shortcut through your field? I have to catch the 8:45 train."

The farmer smiled, "Go ahead, young feller, but if my new bull sees you, you'll probably catch the earlier one at 7:55!"

· ·

A young man walked into a store that advertised a 24-hour turnaround for developing pictures.

"When can I pick up the finished pictures?" the young man asked.

"Thursday will be fine," the store manager said.

"Thursday?" the young man gasped. "You have a sign in the window that says 24-hour service!"

"That's true," replied the manager. "We work eight hours on Monday, eight hours on Tuesday and eight hours on Wednesday. Yup, your pictures will be ready Thursday. Have a good day!"

· ·

A young man went to a very fashionable office for a job. As he was being interviewed, the employer asked, "And as part of our inquiry into the IQ of the people who work for us, could you tell me what the term '*Aurora Borealis*' means?"

The young man, completely baffled, thought for a moment, then said sadly, "It means 'I don't get the job...'"

Abe and Moe were sitting on a park bench in Brooklyn, passing the idle hours in their retirement.

"Moe, I thought you'd like to know, my annuity just came due and I'm going to get $200 a week from now on."

Abe raised his eyebrows sarcastically and quipped, "*Eh, could be better.*"

Moe took a deep breath, a little annoyed, "And what's more, a cousin just passed away and left me $50,000 in her will."

Abe *shuckled* with his shoulders once more and snapped, "*Eh, could be better.*"

A little exasperated, Moe continued, "Also, I forgot to tell you they just notified me from the Irish Sweepstakes that I won the first prize of $100,000!"

Abe again *shuckled* with his shoulders and quipped, "*Eh, also it could have been better.*"

In exasperation Moe turned to him and snapped, "What you talking? Everything by you could be better! What do you know?"

"What could be better, you ask?," quipped Abe, "It could have happened to me instead of you!"

• •

Abe called Western Union and said, "Lady, I want to send a telegram to Moe Schwartz, on Schenectady Avenue, in Brooklyn." The telegram operator said, "Excuse me sir, could you please spell the street for me?"

The old timer sighed and said, "Lady, if I could spell the street, I would be writing the letter myself!"

. . . .

All the umbrellas that were used in emergencies at a certain yeshiva were damaged. Chaim, the attendant, finally decided to take them all in to a friend on the Lower East Side who promised to repair them at no cost.

A few days later, Chaim was on the subway riding to his friend's store to pick them up, and, as he got up to leave the train, out of habit he mistakenly picked up the umbrella that belonged to a lady sitting next to him.

"Stop! Thief!" the lady screamed as she chased him to retrieve her umbrella. Chaim apologized profusely and tried to explain it was a mistake, but the lady went back onto the train in a huff, shrugging, "A likely story!"

Chaim went to his friend's shop, picked up the six umbrellas and took the subway back to the yeshiva. He sat down on the train, and sure enough, the same lady who had been seated next to him was on the same train.

Seeing the six umbrellas under his arm, she turned to him and commented snidely, "You certainly had a good day, didn't you?"

. . . .

An apartment house in the Bronx had been robbed so many times that the tenants formed a protection committee and erected a sign. It read:

"NOTICE TO THIEVES: YOU ARE TOO LATE. OTHER THIEVES HAVE ALREADY ROBBED THESE PREMISES. THERE IS NOTHING OF VALUE LEFT TO TAKE."

Two days later, somebody stole the sign.

. . . .

An old spinster school teacher walked into a chicken market in Brooklyn and said to the butcher, "Pardon me. I want to buy a chicken, but I'm very particular, you know."

The butcher smiled with pride, "Everyone of my chickens is one hundred percent perfect! Go to the chicken coop, pick out the bird you want and we'll have it processed and cleaned for you in less than an hour."

The woman walked over to the coop, selected one bird, then squeezed its stomach, tugged at its feathers, checked its wings, examined its legs, its beak, its toe nails, its eyes…everything you could imagine. Then, very haughtily, she turned to the butcher and declared, "I'm sorry, your bird does not live up to my standards. It does not pass my examination!"

The butcher sighed in exasperation, "Lady, and who could?"

. . . .

An old timer was in the Long Island Railroad station. As the train pulled into the station he asked the conductor, "Does this train stop at Atlantic Avenue?"

The conductor replied, "That's the last stop. If it doesn't, you sure are gonna hear a loud crashing sound!"

An old timer was sitting on a bench in Central Park when his friend walked by and sat down. Together they mused about life and politics, and ate their lunch from a paper bag.

Then, one of the old timers put his hands behind his back and playfully asked his friend, "I have a riddle for you. I am holding in my hands something that starts with an 'H.' Can you guess what it is?"

His friend thought and thought and then announced, "I know what it is. It's a happle."

The old timer shook his head and said, "It starts with an 'H' but it's not a happle"

This friend furrowed his brow, thought, and smiled. "I know! It must be a horange!"

The old timer smiled, "No, it starts with an 'H' but it's not a horange!"

Now the friend was stumped. "I give up!"

The old timer opened his hands and said triumphantly, "See, I fooled you, it's hempty!"

• •

An old timer was walking down the street when he saw a mean looking dog in front of him and a little kid standing by the dog's side.

"Does your dog bite?" the man asked.

"No, sir," the youngster replied.

Just then, as the man tried to pass, the dog jumped up and snapped at the man.

The man shouted indignantly, "You just said your dog doesn't bite!"

The little kid sighed, "It doesn't! This is not my dog!"

· ·

An old timer was walking along Broadway when he was stopped by a missionary, who said, "I am collecting for the L-rd."

The old timer smiled and declared, "Son, I am much older than you and I will probably see the L-rd before you do. I'll give it to Him personally. Thank you."

· ·

An organization invited a rather prominent lawyer to address the group. The lawyer spoke for more than two hours. At the end of the speech one of the attendees walked over to the attorney and said, "Your talk was terrible! I was never so bored in my life!"

The president of the organization blushed embarrassingly and turned to the lawyer. "Please don't pay any attention to him. He's a known *nudnik* and doesn't know what he is talking about; he only repeats what everybody says."

· ·

An out-of-towner stops by a shul and asks if anyone there knows the shul's president, Seymour Rabinowitz.

One man walks forward and says, "Rabinowitz? That scoundrel? That crook? That no-*goodnik?*"

The stranger, aghast, asks, "How come you know so much about him?"

The old-timer smiled. "How come? Because I'm his best friend!"

. . . .

Cohen called a ticket office and tried to buy tickets to a concert. "I'm sorry, sir," the ticket clerk said, "All the tickets are sold out."

Cohen thought for a moment, then asked, "Tell me, if the president of the United States wanted to see the show, would you be able to find a ticket for him?"

The clerk replied, "Of course we'd find a ticket for the president."

Cohen breathed deeply and said, "Well, look, I have it from reliable sources that the president won't be in town the night of the concert, so how about selling me the ticket you would have found for him?"

. . . .

Cohen got a call from a deadbeat relative who was constantly calling him for loans.

"Hello, Shmuel? Listen, could you loan me $20?"

"All right," Cohen sighed, "Come over and I'll help you out again."

In a few minutes the relative was at Cohen's door. Cohen put his hand in his pocket and handed him $10.

"Hey, wait a minute!" the relative complained, "I asked for $20!"

Cohen shrugged, "Look, I'll lose $10 and you'll lose $10, alright?!"

. . . .

Cohen needed a shipping clerk, so he called an agency and they sent over a young man.

"Do you have any experience?" Cohen asked.

"Yes," replied the young man. "I was with Goldberg and Goldberg for five years in their shipping department."

Cohen excused himself and went to a phone to call Goldberg and Goldberg.

"Hello, Goldberg?" he said. "I have a young man here who says he was with your firm. His name is Moscowitz. How long did he work for you?"

Goldberg replied, "About two weeks."

"What?" Cohen shrieked. "He said he was with your firm for five years!"

"That's true," replied Goldberg, "But you asked me how long he *worked* for me. All the time he was with us, he worked for maybe two weeks, and that's why he isn't here anymore!"

Cohen went down for lunch. As he carried his tray to his table, he spotted Rosenberg, who owed him some $500 for merchandise for more than a year.

Cohen realized Rosenberg was in bad financial straits, so he never even asked him for the money. However, a friend is a friend, so he greeted Rosenberg warmly.

"Hello Rosenberg," he said pleasantly. "How are you? The wife, the children?"

"Cohen, you'll get your money! Please stop badgering me."

. . . .

Finkelstein appeared before the Bureau of Naturalization. The clerk looked over his application and then said he would ask him a few questions.

"Mr. Finkelstein, tell me, where is Washington?"

"*Ich vaise?* He's dead!"

"The capitol of the United States, Mr. Finkelstein. Where is it?"

"Oh," purred Finkelstein, "Mostly in Europe!"

"I give up," sighed the clerk. "Look, one more question. Do you promise to support the Constitution?"

"*Nuch dos felt mir!*" cried Finkelstein, "With a wife and six children, how can you expect me to?"

Gedalia explained to his friend, "Gee, I got a wonderful boss! I was getting $10 a week and my boss just doubled my salary."

"Mazel Tov! *Nu*, so what are you getting now?" his friend asked.

"$10 every two weeks!"

• •

Goldberg and Kreisler went into business. A few months later, Goldberg came in and announced, "Sam, I just had my name legally changed to Carson. I think it will help business to have a fancy name like that!"

Sure enough, business happened to improve. A while later, Kreisler came in and announced, "Irving, I also just had my name legally changed to Carson! Now with a business name of 'Carson and Carson,' we have to strike it rich!"

And from that day on, whenever the secretary got a call from a customer who asked to speak to Mr. Carson, she would ask, "Which Carson, Goldberg or Kreisler?"

• •

Goldberg's elderly mother yelled into the phone, "*Gevald!* I've got a skunk in my sukkah!" she complained to the police.

The officer was very comforting, "Lady, don't panic! All you have to do is make a trail of breadcrumbs from inside the

sukkah all the way to your yard and wait a few minutes. The skunk will follow the breadcrumbs out to your yard."

"Oh, thank you so much!" she sighed.

In a few minutes she was back on the phone more frantic than ever.

"What happened?" questioned the police officer.

"I did what you told me," she said, "Now there are four skunks in my sukkah!"

. . . .

Goldberg had made sergeant. The first day he was in charge of the lineup, the Captain called for an inspection. The platoon lined up in front of the barracks, which was spic-and-span, as the Captain walked through their ranks.

When he completed the inspection, he turned to Goldberg and asked, "Very nice Sergeant Goldberg! But, tell me, why have you placed all the tall handsome men in the front ranks while the more homely and short soldiers are in the back?"

Goldberg smiled uneasily and replied, "To tell you the truth, I used to own a fruit store and I forgot myself for the moment."

. . . .

Goldberg operated a small candy store on the Lower East Side. The store was laden with old soda bottles and junk from over the years.

One day, as Goldberg was cleaning up, he rubbed one of

the old bottles and there was a tremendous swishing sound and suddenly a Genie appeared.

"I am the Genie of the soda bottles and have been imprisoned in these bottles for years. Now that you have freed me, I can grant you three wishes!"

Goldberg was flabbergasted but figured why throw away an opportunity? He turned to the Genie and said, "For years I've worked and never have I taken a days vacation. I wish I could be transported to Grossingers for two weeks to rest and enjoy the country air. But who will mind my store?"

The Genie smiled and said, "I will grant your wish and mind your store. But what is your second wish?"

Goldberg thought for a moment and said, "I always wanted a new showcase for the five cent candies that I charge six cents for. I wish I had a new showcase!"

The Genie smiled and exclaimed, "You shall have a new showcase. And now, what is your final wish?"

"Well, I would like to give my final wish to the next person who comes into the store while I'm gone. My customers have always been so loyal, so I think it would be fitting to give them the final wish."

"It shall be done, Master," exclaimed the Genie.

Suddenly there was a swish and a new showcase appeared. Then there was another swish and Goldberg was transported to Grossingers for his two-week vacation. The Genie put on an apron and got behind the counter. Sure enough, the door opened and in walked Finkelberg, Goldberg's best customer.

"Where's Goldberg?" he asked.

"He's gone on a vacation," replied the Genie, "And I'm running the store while he's away."

"Oh," exclaimed Finkelberg. "In that case, I wish you'd make me a vanilla smoothie."

And with that there was a big swishing sound and Finkelberg became...a vanilla smoothie."

. . . .

Goldberg walked into his boss's office and declared, "Sir, my wife said I was to ask you for a raise!"

The boss looked up and replied, "That's wonderful, I'll ask my wife if I can give you one."

. . . .

Goldberg was late for work and raced for the ferry. Just as he reached the pier, he saw a ferry a few feet from the slip. In a burst of speed he made a tremendous leap and miraculously — by inches — landed on the ferry. He brushed himself off and smiled to the passengers who were applauding.

Then one called out, "But why didn't you wait a few minutes, this ferry is coming in!"

. . . .

Goldberg was telling his friend about the pedigreed bird he just bought for $500.

"Does that bird have the necessary paper that would distinguish it as a real pedigreed bird?"

"Listen," Goldberg said, "This bird has such a distinguished pedigree that if he could talk, he wouldn't talk to either of us!"

⋅ ⋅

Goldberg was visiting a friend on Long Island. As he approached the house there was a small sign that read, 'BEWARE OF DOG.'

As he drove a little further, there was a bigger sign that read, 'BEWARE OF DOG.'

As he approached the house carefully, there was an even bigger sign that read, 'NOT RESPONSIBLE FOR INJURY! BEWARE OF DOG!'

As he reached the house, he rang the bell and out came his friend followed by a tiny little dog.

"Do you mean to tell me that little dog keeps strangers away?" the friend asked.

"No," exclaimed the friend, "But the signs do!"

⋅ ⋅

Goldberg was walking down the street one day and saw an old man with a sign which read, "Please help the blind."

As he approached, the old man said, "Could you give me a dime, sir?"

Goldberg put his hand in his pocket to give the old timer a dime, but he noticed the old faker peeking through one eye.

"Hey, are you a wise guy or something? You can see through one eye!"

The old timer shrugged, "Okay, so gimme a nickel!"

. . . .

How about the fellow who worked for a boss for twenty years. Every single day he would be at his little workbench, 20 to 30 minutes before starting time, always doing his best for his boss.

Then it happened.

One day on the way to work, he was run down by a huge truck and was dragged 20 feet. But, thank Heavens, he was not seriously injured.

He raced for his place of business, his clothing torn, his face bleeding and favoring his right foot, which had almost been mangled.

When he arrived, he was just over an hour late.

Sure enough, at the time clock stood his boss with a scowl on his face. He surveyed the ripped clothing, blood-drenched coat and the facial scratches and asked, "What happened to you? Why are you late this morning?"

The poor fellow took a deep breath and was barely able to speak, but managed to say, "I was run down by a huge truck and dragged 20 feet!"

The boss turned away in disgust and snapped, "And that took an hour?"

. . . .

I have two friends — one is crazier than the other. Last summer one of them decided to take a trip to Russia.

"You're crazy," the second fellow exclaimed, "Why Russia?"

"Look, that's my business," the first guy replied.

"If you go, I'll make trouble for you!" threatened the other.

"You'll make trouble for me? Once I'm in Russia what kind of trouble could you make for me?"

"Okay," the second fellow exclaimed, "You'll see."

The first night he was in Russia, his friend sent a cablegram which read, "If you can't get Brezhnev, go for Gromyko!"

. . . .

In one of the Lower East Side restaurants of New York, a man walked in and was approached by a Chinese waiter who asked for his order in perfect Yiddish. The customer was flabbergasted, and pleasantly so.

After he had finished his meal, he passed the owner of the restaurant and exclaimed, "Hey that's fantastic, a Chinese waiter who speaks Yiddish!"

"Sh-h-h-h!" admonished the owner. "Not so loud...he thinks he's learning English!"

Irving had reached that stage in life when he started looking around for a cemetery plot. One day, he came to a cemetery that he thought would serve his needs. The cemetery salesman started showing him around.

"You see, all the prices vary with the location of the grave. However, if you take my advice, you'll take this plot near the lake. Just look at that serene surface, the little ripples in the water and the tiny goldfish swimming around. After 120 years, what more desirable resting place could there be if not next to this lovely little lake?"

The old timer turned angrily and shouted, "What...with my arthritis?"

. . . .

Irving managed to get a job in a shoe store as a substitute for a salesman who went on vacation. A fast-talking Texan walked in and ordered the most expensive pair of shoes in the place.

As he went to the register he exclaimed, "By George, I don't quite have enough cash on me. I'd like the shoes, but all I have with me is $10. Will it be all right for me to bring the rest in tomorrow?"

Irving smiled warmly and said, "Of course it will!"

As the Texan left, the store owner, who was furiously watching the transaction from the back, grumbled, "And what makes you so certain he'll come back tomorrow?"

"Don't worry, I'm a good judge of character. He'll come back tomorrow. I guarantee it!" Irving exclaimed.

"How could you be so sure?" the owner blasted.

"Because I gave him two left shoes." Irving explained.

• •

I rving met a friend in the diamond market who sold him a beautiful, 4 karat, pure-white diamond. On the way home he met his friend Max.

"Did I get a buy!" Irving exclaimed proudly, "I picked up this diamond for $2,000 and it's easily worth $4,000!"

Max looked at the diamond and admitted it was beautiful. "Listen, my daughter is getting married and this would be a wonderful gift. I'll give you $2,200 right now. You'll turn over a $200 dollar profit with no shopping for a buyer."

Irving thought for a moment and agreed. Max gave him the cash and left.

On the way home Irving thought to himself, "If Max offered me $200 on the spot, chances are the diamond is worth ten times that much - after all, Max knows diamonds."

He got off the train and rushed to a phone. "Hello Max, this is Irving. Listen, that diamond I just sold you, I was thinking since it's my wife's birthday next week, I'd like to give her the diamond. Tell you what: I'll give you $2,400 for the diamond. You'll turn over a quick $200 and my Sadie will be happy."

"It's a deal," snapped back Max, and, by the time Irving got home, Max was at his house to turn over the diamond and get the cash.

On the way home Max thought, "Aha! Irving must know something. If he offered me $200 extra for that diamond, it must be worth at least ten times that amount, because he knows nothing about diamonds." He quickly ran to the phone and called Irving.

"Listen, my daughter was heart-broken when I told her what I did, so I'll give you $2,600 for the diamond if you give it back."

Irving impulsively snapped, "It's a deal!" and in ten minutes, he was back at Max's house with the diamond to pick up the cash.

On the way home, Irving felt pangs of regret. "Max sure knows how to drive a hard bargain. If he is already paying $600 more for that diamond, it certainly must be worth a hundred times that amount!" When he reached his house, he ran to the phone and called Max.

"Max, I changed my mind. I'll take the diamond back" Before he could finish, Max interrupted, "You're too late, I just gave it to my daughter!"

"How could you do such a thing, Max, when we were both making such a wonderful living from that diamond?"

. . . .

Irving walked into his boss's office and asked for a raise. "Could you give me two good reasons why I should give you a raise?" snapped his boss.

"Sure," replied Irving, "My wife and my mother-in-law!"

Isn't it true that the shortest distance between two points is always under construction?

• •

It was a children's concert and each of the little ones stepped up to the piano to play their selection. By the time the tenth one played, there was an old-timer sitting in the front row brushing away tears from his eyes.

The music teacher leaned over and whispered, "You really must be touched by the children. Are you a parent?"

The old timer tried to smile, "No, I'm a musician!"

• •

It was a dark dreary night. The wind was howling and the sky was overcast. Sarah couldn't sleep. Suddenly, there was a bolt of lightning which lit up the sky. The figure of a burglar was outlined in the window.

"Shloimy! There's a burglar standing by the window!"

Stirring slowly, Shloimy stared bleary eyed through his sleep and spied the burglar and his burglar tools just outside the window.

"Sh-h-h-h-h," he cautioned. "Don't scare him. Maybe he can get the window up. That's the one we couldn't get open since the painters left!"

It was at the opening of the Philharmonic at Lincoln Center. Sam Alrightnick, in an effort to instill culture in his wife Becky, picked up two tickets.

When they got to the concert hall, by coincidence, they sat next to Becky's neighbor, Shirley. Each was bursting with pride to be seen by the other.

Finally, the conductor came out on stage and the symphony began. The orchestra played brilliantly. Cymbals crashed. The sound of the brass filled the auditorium. Then suddenly, as the percussion crescendo increased, there came a sudden halt. It was a rest in the music where every instrument ceased for a second.

From the rear of the auditorium Becky's voice echoed. "Then you grate in a few onions and let it simmer…"

· ·

It was autumn and the Indians on a remote reservation asked their new Chief if the winter was going to be cold or mild. Since the new Chief had never been taught the old secrets and couldn't tell from looking up at the sky what the weather was going to be, to be on the safe side, he told his tribe that the winter was, indeed, going to be cold and that they should collect as much wood as they could to be prepared.

But, being a practical leader, after several days, he got an idea. He went to a phone booth and called the National Weather Service and asked if the coming winter was going to be cold.

The meteorologist replied, "Yes, the winter will be quite cold!" So, the chief went back to his people and told them to collect even more wood in order to be prepared.

A week later the Chief called the National Weather Service again and asked, "Is it really going to be a cold winter?"

The meteorologist said, "Yes, absolutely! It will probably be one of the coldest winters we have ever had!"

The chief asked, "How are you sure?"

The meteorologist replied, "Well for one thing, we have been told the Indians are collecting wood like crazy!"

. . . .

It's really easy to identify people who can't count to ten. They're the ones in front of you in the supermarket Express Lane marked, '10 ITEMS OR LESS.'

. . . .

Kelly was crossing a street when he was struck down by a bus. Pretending to be seriously injured, he immediately sued the bus company for a million dollars, claiming he was paralyzed and couldn't ever walk again.

The case went to court and he won. "We're rich! It's a miracle!" he shouted to his wife as they sat in the courtroom.

"But what good is this miracle?" his wife sighed, "The insurance company still thinks you were faking, and the judge, I'm sure, knows you were faking, and both the insurance company and the judge are going to keep an eye on you if

you so much as take a single step. Then they will get you for perjury and fraud!"

Kelly whispered to his wife, "Don't you worry. First, I want you to hire an ambulance. They will wheel me out in a wheelchair. Then they will take us to an airplane that will take us to Israel. When we get to Israel, you will hire another ambulance to take me to the Western Wall, and then, boy are you going to see a miracle!"

. . . .

Last week I dialed a number expecting to get my friend. All of a sudden, a woman's voice answered the phone.

"Excuse me," I said, "Can I speak to Fred?"

"I'm sorry," the voice declared, "There's no Fred here. You must have the wrong number."

"Gee," I exclaimed, "Are you sure there's no Fred there?"

There was a pause on the phone, then the voice answered, "Listen, have I ever lied to you?"

. . . .

Leopold Stokowski was giving a testimonial dinner to his first violinist, a man who had served faithfully under Stokowski's baton for more than twenty years.

At the dinner, Stokowski got to his feet and began to speak. "Mr. Feldberg, for years I have watched you play, and each time the expressions on your face told a story. You would grimace and then show great signs of agony during certain movements, and at one time, I even noticed you crying. I guess it wouldn't be telling any stories out of class if you could explain this.

"I assume the feeling you have for music overcomes you and fills you with such great compassion that you are so overwhelmed, you cannot hold back the agony and emotion that fills you. When tears come to a man's eyes when he plays such great music, there must be a reason. Can you please tell us?"

The old timer looked at Stokowski and explained, "To tell you the truth, I don't like music!"

. . . .

Little Irving was playing in the yard when a neighbor asked him, "Where's your brother?"

"He's inside singing a duet," replied the little one. "With whom?" asked the lady.

"With me," replied the little fellow.

"Then what are you doing here?" she questioned.

"Oh," smiled the little one, "I finished first!"

. . . .

Little Rivka was practicing the piano, when the door bell rang. Sandra's mother went to open the door.

"I'm the piano tuner," a man exclaimed.

"The piano tuner?" she questioned. "I didn't send for a piano tuner."

"I know," replied the tuner, "But the neighbors did."

* *

Little Shloimy walked into the Police Station and said, "I want to report my puppy dog missing."

The desk officer smiled and said, "There's really nothing we can do. Why don't you hang up signs or put an ad in the newspaper?"

The little one sighed, "He's just a puppy. He can't read yet!"

* *

Mr. Goldberg proudly announced, "My son, Seymore, is going away to Europe to study singing."

"Thank heavens!" replied the upstairs neighbor.

* *

Mrs. Feinberg and her little son are about to get on a bus. She tells the little one, "If the driver asks you your age, tell him you are only five years old. This way, I won't have to pay for you."

When they boarded the bus, the driver looked at the youngster and asked, "How old are you?"

The little one replied, "I'm only five years old."

The driver was a little suspicious and asked, "And when are you going to be six?"

The little one smiled and replied, 'When I get off the bus."

Mrs. Goldberg was talking with her painter concerning the wallpaper to be hung in her kitchen. After half an hour of looking through a swatch book, the painter asked, "Tell me, Mrs. Goldberg, would you like a border?"

Mrs. Goldberg smiled sweetly and replied, "Thank you, but I have enough taking care of my own family."

One day, Sam ran after the garbage truck yelling, "Am I too late for the garbage?"

The driver called back, "No, jump in!"

One of the great classic stories told about a tailor concerned the old timer who was an excellent tailor but always walked around in tattered clothes. One day in shul, the rabbi asked him, "Mottel, you sew beautifully. You make magnificent clothing for everybody in our village, yet your clothes are in tatters. Why don't you at least fix your pants and jacket so that you'll look a little more respectable when you come to shul?"

The little tailor sighed, "Oh, I wish it were so. You see, I am so poor that every spare moment I have, I must work for payment, otherwise I would starve."

The rabbi put his hand in his pocket and handed him a $5 bill. "Here, take this and make believe I am your customer. Now, I want you to go back to your tailor shop and repair your clothing. Remember, you are doing this for money so you can't think you are squandering your time."

Mottel took the money and went home. The following day in shul, Mottel appeared with his clothing still in tatters.

"Mottel," asked the rabbi, "I gave you $5 to fix your pants and jacket, and they are still just as torn and ragged as before. Why?"

Motel sighed innocently and replied, "Rabbi, I know you are an understanding person. You see, when I took the $5, I had every intention of repairing my clothing, but when I got back to the shop and began to work on the pants, I discovered there was so much work involved that I honestly could not do it for just $5! So here's your $5 back. Maybe you can find a tailor who could do the job for $5 — for me it doesn't pay."

. . . .

One of the neighbors was holding a Bar Mitzvah reception on her lawn. But through an error, she forgot to send an invitation to a neighbor who lived a few doors away. Realizing the mistake, the woman went over to the neighbor and apologized.

"Please forgive me, Mrs. Finkelstein, I overlooked sending you the invitation, but we do want you to come."

"I'm sorry," exclaimed Mrs. Finkelstein coldly, "I won't go."

"Why?" pleaded the lady.

"Because," exclaimed Mrs. Finkelstein, "It's too late!"

"What do you mean, too late?" pleaded the lady.

"Because," exclaimed Mrs. Finkelstein, "I already prayed for rain..."

. . . .

One poor soul who was trying to get out of Russia finally appealed to the manager of a traveling circus to help him. "Well, our gorilla died last night. But, if you really want to leave, we have a gorilla suit that you can wear. You put on the suit and get into the gorilla's cage. We'll be leaving Russia tomorrow night."

The man thanked the circus manager, put on the gorilla suit and got into the gorilla's cage. That night, as the circus caravan lumbered toward the Russian border, one of the bars that separated the gorilla's cage from the lion's cage fell out.

The lion, seeing the opening, began to claw his way through the small opening, trying desperately to get into the gorilla's cage. The man in the gorilla suit began to scream, "Help! Help!"

Just then, the lion called out, "Quiet! You think you're the only one who's trying to get out of Russia?"

. . . .

Rabbi Goldberg was taking his evening constitutional down the avenue when he came upon little Seymour, standing on tip-toe, trying to reach the doorbell.

"Hello Seymour," the rabbi greeted the youngster.

Recognizing the child was trying to reach the doorbell, the rabbi said, "Let me help you."

The child waited until the rabbi had pushed the buzzer and then shouted, "Thank you rabbi! Now we run!"

. . . .

Rabinowitz cried out to the desk sergeant at the police station, "Quick! Quick! Put me in jail. I got into an argument and I lost control of myself and I whacked my friend with a frying pan."

"Did you kill him?" questioned the sergeant.

"No!" exclaimed Shloimy, "That's why I want you to lock me up!"

. . . .

Returning home from shopping, a young homeowner was shocked to find that her house had been ransacked and burglarized. She phoned the police and reported the crime.

The police dispatcher broadcast the call on all channels and a K-9 unit patrolling nearby happened to be the first on the scene.

As the K-9 officer approached the house with his dog on a leash, the woman ran out on the porch, clapped her hands to her head and moaned, "*Oy gevald!* I come home and find all my possessions stolen. I call the police for help and what do they do? They send a *blind* policeman!"

Rosenberg had just graduated from the Police Academy and was assigned one of the toughest neighborhoods in Brooklyn. As he was walking his beat the very first night on assignment, a big, tough anti-Semite stepped in front of him and tauntingly growled, "Pig!"

"Rosenberg," smiled the officer, as he walked on.

. . . .

Rosenberg was more than a little annoyed when his neighbor, Lapidus, telephoned him at 3:00am, screaming into the phone, "Your dog is barking so loudly, I can't sleep!" Rosenberg slammed the phone down before Lapidus could even finish speaking.

The next day Rosenberg called Lapidus at 3:00am and shouted into the phone, "Lapidus, I don't own a dog!"

. . . .

Sadie Cohen lived in an integrated neighborhood on Long Island. Her neighbor was a very generous gentile woman who stopped in one Saturday morning and asked, "Mrs. Cohen, I have to go into New York City this afternoon to meet my daughter. Can I get you anything?"

Mrs. Cohen thanked her and exclaimed, "Listen, I have a commuter's ticket for the train. Why don't you use my ticket and you'll bring it back tonight. After all, it's all paid for; why should you pay extra?"

The neighbor thanked her and got on the train. As the

conductor came through the train he happened to glance at the ticket and noticed the name, Sadie Cohen.

"Excuse me, madam," the conductor declared, "Are you Sadie Cohen, the person whose name appears on this ticket?" The woman smiled sweetly and shook her head affirmatively.

A little suspicious, he asked, "Then let me compare signatures. Would you please sign your name?"

The gentile lady turned indignantly and snapped, "You want me to write on Shabbos?"

* *

Sadie Goldberg was walking along Fifth Avenue and stopped into one of those ultra-fancy confectionery cookie shops that advertised kosher cookies. This was the last word in expensive and elegant delicacies — rugs on the floor, plush couches lining the walls, stereo music filtering through the place. Sadie approached the counter as a fancily dressed woman came over to wait on her.

"Good afternoon," the saleswoman began, "It is a pleasure to serve you, madam. What would be your pleasure?"

Sadie was taken aback by all this elegance and merely pointed to some cookies in the showcase. "If you'll be so kind, I'll take a pound of the small crackers with the chocolate icing."

The saleswoman stood back, aghast. "Madam, p-u-l-l-e-e-z-z-, here we call them 'Petit fours.' One pound, you said. Will there be anything else?"

Sadie looked for a moment, then pointed to another delicacy and said, "Also, I'll take a pound of the chocolate candy."

The saleslady was beside herself. "Madam, please in here we call them 'Bon Bons.' As you know, we have an exclusive clientele...."

Sadie nodded apologetically.

"And where shall we have it delivered?" the saleslady asked softly.

"Why bother?" Sadie exclaimed. "Listen, I'm taking the subway on the corner and two pounds of cookies I can carry."

"You don't understand," the saleslady explained once more, "There is no charge for our service. In fact, our establishment prides itself in its service. However, if you wish to take it with you — and it is a little irregular — I'm sure we can accommodate you."

"Thank you," Sadie exclaimed, "I don't mind carrying it."

The saleslady smiled warmly and concluded, "Why schlep in this heat, right?"

. . . .

Sadie was expecting company and set out the fancy guest towels. To make sure the kids didn't use those towels until the guests arrived, she scribbled a note, which read, "If you use these towels, I will be very upset!" She placed the note on the towel rack, confident the kids would take heed. She then went about straightening up the house and forgot about the note.

The next day, after the guests had left, Sadie was beside herself when, while straightening up the washroom, she found the forgotten note still there and all the towels untouched.

Sam had struck it rich and was now moving in high society. One day, he was invited to attend a very fancy dinner with his wife. They dressed for the occasion and were well received. As the conversation moved on, one of the cultured women asked Sam's wife, "Mrs. Rosenberg, what do you think of Omar Khayyam?"

His wife smiled and replied, "Personally, I like Kedem wine better. It's a little sweeter." A few eyebrows were raised but no one said a word, wishing not to embarrass her. The women quickly changed the subject and the evening went on without any deep conversation.

On the way home, Sam snapped at his wife. "When are you going to learn? Don't you know Omar Khayyam is not a wine! It's a cheese!"

• •

Sam is walking down the street and meets his friend Irving. "Hello, Irving," Sam exclaimed, "Boy is that a suit you have on. It's beautiful!"

"I'll give you the name of my tailor. Very expensive, but exclusive!"

Sam gave him the address and he quickly went to the little store on the Lower East Side. He walked in and told the tailor he wanted a suit just like his friend. The tailor responded, "You know, by me I get $800 for a suit!"

"Eight Hundred dollars for a suit? Why? How?" exclaimed Irving.

"Well," the tailor began, "I first have to call a friend in Japan where the silk worms must start to make up the lining for the jacket. You know the little worms must put in overtime for such a fine jacket. Then, I have to call a friend in Africa to have him smuggle out little pieces of ivory for the buttons. They have little Pygmies who carve the buttons all day long. They have to get paid. And then I must put a call to Australia for another friend to send up wool for the garment. Then I have to put all the parts together and set up the suit."

"Aha," sighed Irving, "Now I know why you must get so much for a suit. But tell me, if I ordered one today, when could I get it?"

The little tailor figured and figured, then exclaimed, "You'll come tomorrow around 3:00pm, I'll have it ready."

· ·

Sam met his old friend Goldblatt. "*Nu*, Goldblatt, how's by you?"

Goldblatt shrugged, "*Eh...*"

Sam sighed, "And the store — it's doing okay?"

Goldblatt sighed, "*Eh...*"

"*Nu*, and the wife and children?" Sam asked.

Goldblatt groused once more, "*Eh...*"

Sam smiled warmly as he shook the old timer's hand, "It's such a pleasure to meet an old friend and have a heart to heart conversation!"

Sam Ousgeshpilt was a poor and lonely tailor who barely made enough money to support himself in his tiny little shop. He would work from morning to night slaving over the pressing machine, sewing until the wee hours of the morning and doing whatever he could to earn a living.

He had one little vice that gave him a ray of hope. That was the Sweepstakes ticket he would purchase every year. Each week, Sam would put away 25 cents from his meager earnings, just so he could buy a ticket and have something to hope for from day to day.

Then one day, it happened. The door of his tiny shop opened and in walked a very well dressed man who told Sam he had won the first prize of one million dollars in the Irish Sweepstakes!

Sam was so overcome with emotion he didn't know what to say. He quickly closed his shop, moved into a fancy hotel, bought a wardrobe that could have stocked a department store and began a new life. He went to fancy clubs, bought a huge yacht and began sailing around the world. Every night it was the same thing, he would drink himself silly and stay up until all hours of the night.

By the end of the fifth month, his health began to show the effects of this fast living, yet he didn't stop. He continued living high, and finally, by the end of the year, he found that he didn't have a penny left to his name.

His new fair-weather friends left him and he was barely a shell of a man. His health had been ruined, his life was a mess and he had practically no means of support.

Finally, he remembered the little tailor shop. Through the help of an old friend, he was able to reopen his shop once more and go back to work.

Once more, he toiled from morning until night. He continued in the same pattern he had set for himself before he had won the Sweepstakes prize money.

Through force of habit, he began to put away a 25 cents every week to save for the Sweepstakes ticket. He really didn't believe that he could win again; after all, how often could lightning strike the same person?

Sure enough, after a few months, the door of his little shop opened and in walked another well-dressed man who announced, "Sam, you have just won first prize again in the Irish Sweepstakes! Here's a check for one million dollars. Congratulations!"

Sam looked up from his pressing table, put his hands to his head, and, remembering the past year, shrieked, "*Oy vey!* Do I have to go through all that again?"

. . . .

Sam was let go from his job because he simply couldn't do the work. However, the boss didn't want to hurt him so he told him he was simply laid-off.

A few days later, Sam located another job and needed a letter of recommendation. His boss wrote, "Sam Goldberg worked for me for six months — and then he left me. We were perfectly satisfied!"

Sarah and Effy lived in a comfortable apartment in Brooklyn. But Sarah wasn't satisfied. She kept nagging her husband, day in and day out, for them to move to a more expensive apartment.

"We could afford it!" she exclaimed. "After these years of skimping and saving we're entitled to a little luxury."

"But I like it here," Effy explained. "Why move to a more expensive apartment?"

This went on for months. Then finally, one night, Effy came home and exclaimed, "Sarah, you will finally get your wish. Starting next month, we'll be living in a more expensive apartment!"

"Oh, that's wonderful!" Sarah cried. "Did you find a place in a nice neighborhood?"

"Not quite," sighed Effy. "I just met the landlord downstairs and he said he's raising our rent starting next month!"

. . . .

Seymour Goldberg bought a ticket to a show. When he looked at his change, he ran back to the ticket booth. "Excuse me, Miss," he said. "I think you made a mistake in my change."

The girl, a very snooty individual, scowled and looked at him with anger.

"Sir," she began, "The policy of this theater is to handle all transactions at the time of the ticket sale. You should have counted your change the moment I gave it to you. I cannot possibly remember the amount of change I gave a purchaser. How do I know you wouldn't be cheating me with your accusations? I'm sorry, there isn't a thing I can do. If there was a mistake, then it's a mistake and that's that!"

Seymour sighed as he walked away, "I only wanted to tell you that you gave me twenty dollars too much change."

. . . .

Shapiro was riding on the subway when he noticed to his amazement a man sitting opposite him with two pigeons on his shoulders. "That's fantastic," he muttered to himself. "The control of those pigeons sitting on a man's shoulder with all this noise and confusion is just astounding!"

Finally, he couldn't control himself and approached the man. "Pardon me, but I just had to tell you those are wonderful pigeons you got there. Where did you get them?"

The little old timer looked up very unconcerned and exclaimed, "*Ver veis?* (Who knows?)...they got on at the last stop."

. . . .

Shapiro was talking to his employees. "I want you to know I am a very fair person. I want you to speak your mind any time something bothers you - just come to my office and tell it to me straight — even if it costs you your job."

hloimy was active in Mayor Lindsay's campaign and, as a reward, he was given a junior commissionership in the traffic department. He was a *noch-schlepper* (a tag-along of not much value).

Since the heads of the traffic department realized Shloimy was just supposed to be a fixture there for a few weeks, they told him to sit down at a desk and figure out how to solve New York City's traffic problem.

Shloimy pondered the question all of ten minutes, then ran into the Commissioner's office with the startling assertion, "Gentlemen, I have solved the traffic problem in New York City!"

The Commissioner pushed back his chair and looked curiously at the map Shloimy held in his hand. It was a block-by-block detailed map of the city's arteries.

Suddenly, the Commissioner turned from the map and declared, "My good man, do you see what you've done? You have all the streets in Manhattan going west. What could that possibly accomplish?"

"Listen," exclaimed Shloimy, "If you put that plan into effect on Monday, by Wednesday, the whole problem will be New Jersey's!"

. . . .

hloimy somehow or other got into the prize-fighting business. When his first big fight came, he got into the ring. His opponent sent a quick right swing to his jaw and Shloimy went down to the canvas.

The referee started to count, "One...two...three..." Shloimy's manager leaned over and whispered, "Don't get up till nine!"

Shloimy opened one eye and moaned, "What time is it now?"

· ·

Shloimy was talking to a friend. "You know, it is getting so bad I think I'm going to have to move."

"Why? What happened?" his friend asked.

"What happened? Last night at 4:00am, my upstairs neighbor started banging on the floor with a broom and began stamping his feet like the building was going to cave in."

His friend gasped, "*Nu* — so what did you do?"

"Nothing," Shloimy said. "I just ignored him and continued playing my saxophone."

· ·

Sol Gilman, the wealthy contractor and builder, was looking for a house, and a real estate associate of his called him to come down and look at a place he felt would be ideal for the Gilmans.

"Sol, just look how ideal the location is — right on the bank of the river! Two steps back from the door and you're in the water ready for a swim. Or, still better, you can go fishing right out of your first-floor window. Believe me, Solly, the place is perfect for you!"

"Wel-l-l-l," drawled Gilman, "One thing worries me — suppose the bay overflows its banks?"

The real estate salesman smiled warmly and said, "Sol, how could that possibly affect your house? It's so far from the water!"

. . . .

The economy had slipped and was getting worse. Sam, a clothing store proprietor, had three prime creditors who were screaming for their money. In desperation, he consulted his brother-in-law.

"I need a plan for how to deal with my creditors once and for all. I can't keep hiding from them forever!"

"Okay, I think I have a way out for you. Now, do what I say, it is for your own good!"

"Absolutely, I will follow your advice to the letter," the panic-stricken clothier agreed.

"First, I have to notify the newspapers that you died of a heart-attack quite suddenly. We'll hold a mock funeral, and if everything goes as planned, your financial troubles will be over."

The undertaker, who was in on the plan, gave Sam something that would make his body inert so that he would appear dead, and soon, Sam was lying in his coffin in the funeral parlor as friends, business associates and creditors filed by to pay their respects.

The first creditor was in tears. "Sam...how could you do it?'

he moaned, You only owed me a few thousand. I would have written it off, forgiven everything. You've broken our hearts!"

The second creditor was equally grief-stricken. "You could have come to me for any amount," he said, "I would have set you up in business, Sam — what a loss you are!"

The third creditor stood at the casket and said, "You louse! You cost me my savings, my home, the money for my kids' education. I trusted you and you sent me to the wall. You may be dead, but just the same, I'm going to strangle you to make sure you're truly dead once and for all!"

Sam opened one eye just a slit and whispered, "*You* I'll pay!"

* *

The phone rang in a local hospital and the nurse answered. A voice asked, "Hello, could you please tell me how Mr. Rabinowitz is?"

The nurse replied, "Well, I have his chart here and the doctor says he is doing beautifully. In fact, he says he will be able to go home in a few days. Who shall I say called him?" "Me, Rabinowitz! My doctor treats me like an idiot and tells me nothing! Thank you!"

* *

The recession had hurt Goldberg's business. When his friend entered his little shop, Goldberg was wringing his hands in despair. With tears flowing from his eyes, he turned to his friend and declared, "Sam, I'm bankrupt. I owe everybody!"

Sam tried to console him and said softly, "Listen, Goldberg, it could be worse."

Goldberg bristled, "What are you talking about it could be worse? How? I owe almost everybody!"

Sam sighed, "I might have been one of your creditors."

. . . .

The sign above the door read: "Wong Su — Great Chinese Mystic."

A woman approached the door, rang the bell, and was greeted by an elegantly dressed oriental man.

"Welcome to the sanctuary of the Great Wong, mystic of the Seven worlds. You wish to consult with Wong Su, the great mystic?" the oriental asked solemnly.

"Yes," explained the woman, "Tell him his mother is here from the Bronx."

. . . .

The salesman exclaimed, "This computer will do half your work!"

"Great!" exclaimed the customer, "I'll take two!"

. . . .

There's a cute story told about a Gentile couple who walked into a brand new Chinese restaurant. The husband, who wanted to show his worldliness to his wife, called to the waiter,

"This is our anniversary. Money is no object. Bring us the dish of the house — the thing you make the most of and sell the most of. The one dish you are noted for!"

The Chinese waiter smiled knowingly and disappeared. In a few minutes he was back with a great big sizzling pizza pie.

The young couple looked at the Chinese waiter. "In a Chinese restaurant the dish of the house is a pizza pie? Are you kidding me?"

The waiter snapped back innocently "Whaddya expect? This is a Jewish neighborhood!"

· ·

There's a little Jewish delicatessen on the Lower East Side that has a sign posted near the cashier. It reads, "Customers who think our waiters are rude should see our manager!"

· ·

Three fancy ladies were having tea one afternoon. The first one began, "In this Nuclear Age, we can all be destroyed in a matter of seconds, without having a chance to clear our consciences. So, I will confide my sin to you. Remember when I was president of the Sisterhood? Well, I lost all the money collected that year for the sisterhood by betting it away at the race-track. But no one knew it until now..."

The second woman sighed, "And I, too, have a sin to confess. Nobody knows, but I drink an entire bottle of whiskey every day."

The third woman got up and said, "And my sin is that I'm a terrible gossip and I can't wait to get to a telephone!"

. . . .

Three fellows came racing into Grand Central Station, and just as they got to the gate, it slammed shut. They looked soulfully at the station attendant and asked, "When's the next train?" The attendant answered, "In an hour."

The three turned to each other and agreed they would spend the time in a nearby bar to relax a bit. An hour later, they came racing into the station, but the gate came down just as they arrived and they missed the train a second time.

"When's the next train?" they asked the attendant.

"In another hour," the attendant explained.

The three went back to the bar to finish their repast. In an hour, the three came running into the station, and just as they were reaching the gate, the gate began coming down.

Two of them managed to slip under the gate as it was coming down, but the third one slipped and fell just as the gate slammed shut. The train pulled out with his two friends, but he was left behind.

He sat up and began to laugh hysterically.

"You know, you got a pretty good sense of humor," the station attendant commented. "You tried to get the train three times and missed it all three times. In fact, this time your friends made it and you didn't, yet you can still laugh. That's pretty funny!"

"That ain't what I'm laughing at," the old timer roared. "They came to see me off!"

. . . .

Two bubbies met in the street. "Oy, have I got troubles," sighed the first one.

"What happened," the second one asked.

"I lost everything in the market," the bubby sighed.

"Oh my goodness," the second said. "What happened?"

The first woman nodded soulfully, "My shopping bag broke!"

. . . .

Two fellows were having a drink in a local bar. One of them says, "Hey, did you hear the one about the two Jews who got off a bus and one says to the other..."

The other fellow interrupts, "What's wrong with you? Why must it always be Jews? Why must you always tell stories about Jews? Why don't you pick on some other nationality?"

The friend apologized and continued, "Okay, let me tell you the joke. These two Chinese fellows get off a bus and one says to the other, 'Are you coming to my son's Bar Mitzvah?'"

. . . .

Two friends met on the street. "Abe," the first fellow exclaimed. "I'm so glad to see you. My business is in such

bad shape, it is impossible to survive. In fact, I am so short of cash, I haven't the slightest idea whom to ask."

The second fellow sighed, "I'm glad to hear it...for a minute I thought you were going to ask me."

. . . .

Two garment manufacturers were having an argument. Finally, one partner shouted, "Okay, Levine, I've had it and I want you to know, I'm finally striking back!"

"Oh yeah?" shouted back his partner.

"Yeah!" snapped the first fellow. "To show you what I mean, I just bought my wife a brand new car!"

"*Nu*," the second fellow snapped, "What has that got to do with me?"

"Aha," shouted the first fellow, "Well, my wife is over at your house right now showing it off to your wife. Wait 'till you get home tonight!"

. . . .

Two kids were talking and one said, "You're so dull, I bet you don't know the difference between a trampoline and an accordion!"

The other kid replied, "Oh yeah, I do! You have to take your shoes off before you jump on a trampoline."

Two old time actors, who had worked as a team on the Jewish stage for years, came to loggerheads with each other. Each thought he was better than the other.

"Listen," one partner declared, "I could do Shakespeare, Hamlet and some of the finest plays ever written. I don't have to *schlep* around with a blockhead like you!"

The other hurled back, "Listen Hymie, with my voice, I could sing in the Metropolitan opera and I could be a cantor in the finest shuls - I don't have to take such insults from you."

So the team broke up and each went their separate way. The years passed and no one heard of the other. As it was, Hymie couldn't get a job doing Shakespeare with his thick accent, and Shloimy's voice wasn't as good as he thought.

In desperation, Shloimy took a job as a waiter in a broken down restaurant on the Lower East Side. This was takeh, the last rung on the ladder.

One day, the door opened and in walked his old partner, Hymie. Hymie spotted his old friend and exclaimed, in shock, "Shloimy, you, a man with such great talent, is a waiter in this dirty, filthy, broken down hash house?"

Shloimy cleared his throat and snapped back, "Listen, I'm working a job, but what's your excuse?"

· ·

Two old timers got on a bus in the Catskills and asked the driver, "Does this bus stop at the Pioneer Country Club?"

"No." exclaimed the driver, "We put it in a garage at night."

Two old timers were sitting on a park bench when one of them took a deep breath and sighed "*Oy*, life is just like a cup of tea..."

The second fellow listened intently then questioned, "Life is like a cup of tea? Why?"

The first fellow replied. "How should I know? Am I a philosopher?"

. . . .

Two old timers were walking in the park when it suddenly started to rain.

"Quick, Yankel. Open your umbrella!"

Yankel kept walking and did not even attempt to open the umbrella.

"Yankel, are you crazy? Open the umbrella!" the friend shouted.

Yankel sighed, "It wouldn't do any good. It's all torn and it's broken."

The first fellow shouted, "Then why in the world did you *schlep* the umbrella all the way from your house?"

Yankel sighed once more, "Who thought it would rain?"

. . . .

Two old timers were watching a funeral procession pass down the street. A young man walked over to one of the old timers and exclaimed, "Some crowd! Who died?"

Without batting an eye, the old timer exclaimed, "The fellow in the hearse!"

· ·

Two women met in a supermarket and one turned to the other angrily. "Sara, I can't tell you anything. What I told you yesterday about my personal issues was supposed to be in strictest confidence. Today, it's all over the neighborhood!"

The other woman glared innocently and snapped, "What do you mean I can't keep a secret? It's these big-mouths in the sisterhood I told it to who can't keep their mouths shut! Me? I don't say a word!"

· ·

While visiting family on the Lower East Side, the world-famous violinist, Mischa Elman, volunteered to play the *Kreutzer Sonata* by Beethoven. This is a selection that has a great number of rests interwoven into the theme.

During one of the rest periods, the little old lady who had listened so intently leaned over and whispered to him, "Play something you know, *tateleh!*"

Jewish Wit

. . . .

A Jewish man who owned a small farm in Russia couldn't get men to work for him. It was getting close to the summer planting and in desperation he wrote to his cousin in America.

"I don't know what to do," he complained. "I guess I'll have to dig up the entire four acres in the field myself."

The cousin in America wrote back, "*Oy vey*, don't dig up the fields, that's where the guns are buried!"

The Russian government censored the letter and soon an entire Russian contingent of troops arrived at the property and began digging up every square inch of the field area. Finding nothing, they left.

The cousin wrote once more to America, "Cousin Shloimy, what do I do now? The soldiers dug up every square foot."

Shloimy wrote back, "Now, plant potatoes on the first two acres and corn in the other two!"

• •

A typical story out of Soviet Russia tells of a Communist agent who was taking a census of Jews in a little village. He knocks on one door and calls out, "Does Chaim Novitzky live here?"

A meek little voice from behind the door replies, "No!"

The agent checks his records and calls out, "Then who are you?"

The door opens slowly as an old man in tattered clothing replies, "Me? I'm Chaim Novitzky."

"But you just told me Novitzky doesn't live here."

The old timer shrugs, points to the squalor in his tiny apartment and sighs, "My friend, you call this living?"

• •

A wealthy businessman always liked to kid one of his Jewish employees. One day, he called him into his office and said, "I'm going to put two pieces of paper in a hat. One will be blank, and the other will read $50,000. I will let you pick one piece of paper. If you pick the one with the $50,000, I will give you the money. But if you pick the blank, you will have to give me your next paycheck."

To carry out his joke, the boss secretly didn't mark either piece of paper in order to guarantee that the employee would lose. He placed both pieces of paper in the hat and said, "Pick one."

The employee, suspecting some trickery, picked one little piece of paper, quickly crumpled it up, put it in his mouth and swallowed it.

"Why did you do that?" asked the boss.

"So, you open the piece of paper remaining in the hat, and if that one is blank, then obviously the one I swallowed had the $50,000 written on it. You can give it to me in cash."

• •

A young Yeshiva boy was appearing before an Army induction psychiatrist. The youth was asked how he felt about entering the army.

"Please, kind sir," began the Yeshiva boy. "No matter what happens, don't turn me down! Let me get into a uniform immediately. I can't wait to get into the army. Let me at the enemy. I don't even need a uniform; I'll get them with my bare hands. If they shoot at me, wounded or not, I'll go forward and get them. I'll chew the barbed wire with my bare teeth if necessary. Please let me at them!"

The psychiatrist looked up at the youth and sighed, "Kid, you're crazy!"

The youth looked at the psychiatrist, pointed to the application form on his desk and whispered softly, "Quick, write that down!"

After the Battle of Austerlitz, Napoleon wanted to reward a number of his men who were of different nationalities. All had fought as heroes. Napoleon stepped forward and announced, "Name your wish, gentlemen. Anything you want, I will grant!"

A Polish soldier shouted, "Restore Poland!"

"It shall be done!" shouted Napoleon.

"I'm a farmer — I need land!" a poor Slovak cried.

"And land it will be…" exclaimed Napoleon.

"I want a brewery!" shouted a German soldier.

"We shall get you a brewery…" shouted back Napoleon.

Then a Jewish soldier stepped forward. Napoleon turned to him and asked, "What shall it be my lad — anything you wish!"

The Jewish youth spoke softly, "If you please Sire, I would like to have a kosher pastrami sandwich, with a pickle on the side, and an ice-cold drink…"

"Of course!" shouted Napoleon to one of his men, "Get this man his wish immediately!" A soldier ran out and went in search of a Jewish village where he could procure the desired food. Soon, he came back with the local kosher butcher in tow, who proceeded to give the Jewish soldier a huge, delicious pastrami sandwich and his desired drink.

When the Emperor had left, the others gathered around the Jewish soldier. "What a fool you are! Imagine, the Emperor asked you to wish for anything and all you ask for is a pastrami sandwich? What a fool you are!"

"We'll see who's the fool!" laughed the Jewish soldier. "One of you asked for the independence of Poland, another for a farm, and still another for a brewery — things the Emperor will never get for you. But I'm a realist, I asked for a pastrami sandwich and an ice-cold drink and that I got!"

. . . .

An anti-Semite walked into an appetizing store and said to the owner, "Let me ask you — what makes you Jews so smart?"

The owner, deciding to give this guy the business, leaned over the counter and said, "If you promise not to tell anyone I'll tell you the secret."

The anti-Semite nodded that he would keep the secret.

Cohen whispered, "We eat pickled herring. You see, fish is a brain-food, and when it's pickled, it sharpens the mind. Einstein was a 'three-pickled-herring-a-day' man for years! Let me sell you some. Its only $5 a herring."

The anti-Semite purchased the herrings and left.

Every day he came in, and at $5 a herring, purchased two or three. Then one day he came in and snarled, "Hey, Cohen, I just found out I could get the same pickled herring around the corner for $1 apiece!"

Cohen smiled to him, "See! What did I tell you? See how it's working already?"

Cohen had just come from the store and he was wearing a magnificent suit. His friend, a scholarly gentleman, stopped him and congratulated him on his taste.

"But tell me, I know you earn just a meager living, how could you afford such an expensive suit?" questioned the scholar.

"Well you see," Cohen exclaimed, "Last week, when I went to shul I happened to sit in the sixth seat in the seventh row. Those numbers stuck in my mind. *Nu*, so when a friend of mine said he was going to the race-track, I figured, just for good luck, I was going to use those numbers. I figured six times seven is fifty-one, so I played the five and the one in the daily-double. Sure enough, both horses came in and I won a tidy sum."

The scholar looked at him with disdain. "Hershel Cohen! First, I'm shocked to hear that you gamble; and second, six times seven is not fifty one; it's forty nine!"

Cohen smiled sheepishly and exclaimed, "*Nu*, so you be the accountant!"

. . . .

In an upstate community, there was a police officer who had a reputation for harassing Jewish salesmen. Anytime he could arrest one for selling without a license, he did so. One day, Goldberg happened to be passing through the community. He stopped in a diner to eat when an officer approached.

"What ya' selling?" the officer began.

"Pink Pills for Pale People," Goldberg exclaimed.

"Will ya' sell me $10 worth?" the officer asked.

"Sure," exclaimed Goldberg, and he handed him the pills and accepted the money.

"Aha!" snapped the officer. "Now I got you! Do you have a license to sell in this community?"

"I do," replied Goldberg, and he produced the license. The officer was a little sheepish and said, "Well, now that we've got that settled, what am I gonna do with $10 worth of Pink Pills?"

"Would you like me to buy them back from you?" asked Goldberg.

"Yes. Thanks," replied the officer.

"But all I can give you is $1 for the pills. After all, my business is selling, not buying," Goldberg exclaimed.

The officer hesitated, but figured $1 was better than nothing, so he accepted the dollar and returned the pills.

"Aha!" shouted Goldberg, "Now you're under arrest for selling without a license." And he hauled him off to court where the officer was fined $50!

. . . .

In the days of Czar Nicholas the Second, every Jew was required to have a resident permit. One day, two Jews were walking in the streets of Moscow - one had a resident permit and the other did not. As they turned a corner, they saw a policeman approaching.

"Run!" whispered the one without the permit to the Jew

with the permit. "When the policeman sees you run, he will think you don't have a permit and will start to chase you. While he is chasing you, I will have a chance to get away. If he catches you, show him your permit and nothing will happen to you!"

So, the fellow with the permit began to run. The police officer, seeing the man run, gave chase. As both turned the corner, the fellow without the permit managed to escape.

Finally, after two blocks, the police officer caught up with the fellow who was running. "Aha!" shouted the policeman. "So, I caught you! And, of course, you do not have a permit!"

"No permit?" exclaimed the Jew, "Of course, I have a permit!" He put his hand into his pocket and pulled out the permit.

The policeman was bewildered. "Could you tell me why you started to run when you saw me if you have a valid permit?"

The fellow replied, "My doctor told me to jog a few blocks after every meal, so I was simply jogging!"

"Well, didn't you see me chasing you?" asked the policeman.

"I figured you went to the same doctor!"

• •

Irving the super-salesman walked into a newspaper office and asked the publisher, "Say, do you need a good news editor?"

The publisher said, "No, we have a fine one."

"Well then, could you use a good reporter?" he asked.

"No," replied the editor.

"Well, could you use a good copy-reader or proof-reader?"

"Nope!" replied the editor.

"Then," Irving began, "You certainly need one of these —" From his briefcase he produced a neat metal sign that read, "No Help Wanted!"

• •

Shloimy was fishing in the Catskills with a friend when he noticed the local game warden approaching. He quickly threw his fishing rod to the ground and began to run. When he was a good distance from the fishing spot, the game warden caught up with him.

"Okay," shouted the game warden, "Where's your fishing license?"

Shloimy hesitated for a moment, then reached for his wallet and pulled out a fishing license. The game warden scrutinized it carefully and saw that it was in order.

"Say, why did you run from me? Your license is okay."

Shloimy smiled innocently and explained, "But my friend's isn't!"

• •

The four partners, Tim Murphy, Pat Healy, Jim McKeon and Abe Goldberg had signed a business agreement that should any of them pass away, each would deposit $500 in the grave with the deceased, so that he may venture into another business in the world beyond. It might have been a silly agreement, but the men went along with the idea.

Sure enough, as it must come to all men, Tim Murphy passed on. Following the funeral service, each of the partners passed in front of the casket and carried out their obligation.

First, Pat Healy approached, said a silent prayer, and placed five crisp $100 bills on the coffin. Then Jim McKeon walked over, lowered his eyes and placed $500 in small bills on the coffin. Then Abe Goldberg approached, wrote out a check for $1,500, laid it on the coffin and took $1,000 change.

* *

The president of a large bank became concerned when he saw the delivery boy the bank had recently hired come to work in a chauffeur-driven limousine everyday.

The youth would step out of the car in a $400 suit and go into the bank to take care of his menial job as an inter-office messenger, delivering packages to the various offices in the bank building. The Bank president was curious, so he called the youth into his office one afternoon.

"Goldberg, you're new here, aren't you?" the president asked. The youth nodded, and the president continued. "We noticed you arrive in a chauffeur-driven car every morning. We also know you live in a luxury apartment in New York City, and that you live quite well! We have audited the books and there isn't a penny missing from any of our accounts. I pay you just $150 a week, I earn twenty times that amount and I can barely afford the luxuries you do. Tell me, do you have wealthy parents?"

The youth nodded and said, "No sir. As a matter of fact, I'm an orphan."

"Do you have any endowment or any rich relatives who give you the money to do the things you do?"

The youth shrugged once more. "No sir. The $150 I earn here is my total income."

"Well then, tell me how do you do it?" the president asked.

"Oh, that's easy," exclaimed the youth. "You see, every week I run a raffle for $5. There are more than a hundred employees working in the various offices, and almost every one of them buys a raffle from me. That's how I make my money."

'Good L-rd!" exclaimed the president. "What do you raffle off?"

The youth shrugged, "My $150 paycheck!"

Politics
& High Office

. . . .

A big general who was connected with the Atomic Energy program for military weapons, stopped off in Las Vegas a short time ago and indulged in some of the games. Two Jewish women standing nearby noticed the important officer.

"Sadie," one exclaimed, "Did you see how he's spending his money like there was no tomorrow?"

The other sighed, "Maybe he *takeh* knows something!"

. . . .

A Communist was arguing with a Texan about the functions of democracy. "Listen here," the Texan drawled, "In

America we got such a good democracy that an American could take a train from here - today - and tomorrow be right in Washington, D.C. Once there, he could go to the White House, make an appointment to see the president and then, in a day or so, see the president. He could walk into President Johnson's office and say, "Mr. Johnson, you're a no-*goodnik!*" He could do that and would never be arrested!"

"Well, what you talking," snapped back the Communist, "we can do the same thing in Russia. For example, we could take a train from Minsk to Moscow and, in a few months, we would be in Moscow. Then we would spend months making an appointment to see the Premier. And, after a full investigation, and after being searched a dozen times, maybe three months later we could walk into Mr. Kosygin's office and say, 'Mr. Johnson is a no-*goodnik!*' and believe it or not, we would also not be arrested!"

. . . .

A Communist was arguing with an American, "You communists are all phonies!" exclaimed the American.

"Oh yeah?" snapped the Commie.

"Well, let me ask you: if you had a thousand dollars, would you give me half?" the American asked.

"Sure!" exclaimed the Commie.

"And if you had two cars, would you give me one?" the American asked.

"Of course!" exclaimed the Commie.

"And if you had two shirts would you give me one?" the American asked.

"No!" snapped the Commie.

"Why?" asked the American.

"Because I actually have two shirts," blushed the Commie.

. . . .

A Jew who was rather friendly with some of the higher-ups in the Communist party was asked to make a speech about the wonderful 'freedom' the Jews have in Russia. The old timer was a little hesitant and the Russian Commissar, who was in charge of the propaganda program, warmly put his arm around the Jew and exclaimed, "Listen, comrade, you know in Russia we have freedom of speech, so say what you want."

The old timer looked up sympathetically and exclaimed, "I'm not worried about my freedom to speak; what bothers me is my freedom *after* I speak!"

. . . .

A local candidate was running for office. He had his campaign workers putting up posters and handing out literature, literally working them around the clock. A few days before the election, he decided to call the local delicatessen to order food for an election eve celebration.

"Now listen, Rabinowitz," the candidate shouted into the phone. "Remember, I want you to deliver the food and drinks and set up the tables only if I'm the winner. Do you understand? I'm sending you a check for the full amount, but if for some miraculous reason I am not elected and do not win the election, you are not to bring anything and you will return my check."

"I understand perfectly," said Rabinowitz.

Sure enough, election night came. As the votes started coming in, the candidate sat in a back room with his associates, watching the election results come in, and slowly his small lead began to dwindle away. By 10:00pm, it was quite apparent that he had lost the election.

By 11:00pm, as each of his campaign associates started leaving the room, the candidate walked into the outer hall and was flabbergasted to see all his workers eating the delicatessen he had ordered only if he was the winner. In fact, there was Rabinowitz himself, busily handing out tons of hot dogs and corned-beef sandwiches to the campaign workers.

In anger, the candidate ran over to Rabinowitz and whispered angrily in his ear, "Rabinowitz, are you crazy? I told you to bring the food only if I was the winner. You have a radio and you know I lost by 10,000 votes!"

As Rabinowitz continued serving sandwiches, he turned to the candidate, put his arm around his shoulder and consoled, "Marvin, to *us* you're a winner!"

• •

A local politician was distributing passover packages at a local psychiatric hospital. After he finished distributing the gifts, he wanted to reach his office. He picked up a phone in one of the patient's room. Every time he tried to get a line, he was disconnected. In anger, he dialed the operator and snapped, "Listen, here! I've been trying to get a line for the past ten minutes and you keep disconnecting me!"

The operator said, "Sir, you're not the only one using these phones."

The politician snapped, "Do you know who I am?"

The switchboard operator replied, "No sir, but I do know where you are!"

. . . .

A political polling firm was hired by a politician to see how the vote was going. A representative of the firm was asked to give an oral report to the client, but was warned by his boss, "If the vote looks wrong, be gentle on the client." The young poll-taker said he would take care of it.

When he gave his report, he said, "Well, Sir, as it now stands, you're in great shape! 99% of the voters are for you. The only problem is, I keep running into that 1% who will be voting for your opponent."

. . . .

A politician spoke at a local congregation. After the speech, he asked the president of the shul how he liked the speech. The president said, "Okay, the only problem was with the microphone — it was on!"

A reporter is doing an interview with one of the big generals at Cape Kennedy to find out how accurate our missiles are.

"How accurate are our missiles, general?" the reporter asks.

The general replies, "From Cape Kennedy, we can hit targets in Miami, Fort Lauderdale and Tampa with no problems."

The reporter says, "How about Soviet targets?"

The general says "Of course, if they're located in Miami, Fort Lauderdale or Tampa!"

. . . .

A Republican and a liberal Democrat were arguing politics. The Democrat snapped, "Can you give me any real reason why you are a Republican?"

The Republican snapped back, "Well, my father was a Republican, and his father before him was a Republican, and his father before him was Republican. So that makes me a Republican."

The Democrat snapped back, "Okay, but now answer me this — if your father was morally irresponsible, and his father before him was morally irresponsible, and his father before him was morally irresponsible, what would that make you?"

The other fellow smiled, "Why, that would make me a Liberal Democrat!"

A Russian scientist was recently speaking in Moscow telling his audience, "We Russians are now able to travel to the Moon, Venus, Mars and Saturn."

A little old Jewish man in the back of the auditorium asked softly, "But when will we able to travel to Israel?"

. . . .

A woman was looking out her window as a local politician was making a speech in the street. His followers in the crowd were cheering wildly. Accidentally, the window came down on her back and pinned her partially outside the window. She was locked into that position for nearly half an hour. Finally, she screamed for the police, who came and broke down her door and freed her.

"Lady," the police officer pleaded, "Why did you wait so long to scream and wave your hands to attract attention?"

The old woman smiled sheepishly, "I'm not voting for that candidate, so I didn't want my neighbors to think I was cheering for him!"

. . . .

An American newspaperman was writing to a Russian family. He ended his letter with, "I really doubt whether all the information I have written to you in the above letter will actually reach you, since it is a well known fact that all letters from Americans to Russians are censored."

A few weeks later, the American correspondent got a short

note from Russia. It read, "Dear friend, the closing comment in your letter is an outrageous lie. We do not censor mail from Americans to Russians." It was signed, "The censor."

. . . .

An old Russian Jew was sitting and reading when there was a thunderous knock on the door.

"Who is it?" the old timer asked.

"The KGB!" a voice called out. "Open up!"

The frightened Russian opened the door and the KGB man began to question him. "Comrade, we have reason to believe you are obtaining propaganda literature from Israel. Is that true?"

"Of course not!" the Russian replied indignantly.

"We wish to come in and look around," snapped the KGB man, who suddenly noticed some Hebrew books on the table.

"Why do you have these?" the KGB man shouted.

Shaking with fear the Russian replied, "Because I am learning the Hebrew language..."

"And why are you now learning Hebrew at such an old age?" the KGB man demanded.

"That's just it," sighed the old man. "It's because of my age. I will be meeting my maker quite soon and I am told they only speak Hebrew up there."

Visibly angered, the KGB man shouted, "And what if you go to the other place, you know, down below?"

The old man smiled, "Oh, then there would be no problem because I already speak Russian fluently!"

. . . .

In Washington recently, one of the members of Congress was stopped by a visitor, who asked, "Do you honestly think by giving millions of dollars to underdeveloped nations who are in the Communists hands, the United States is really making friends?"

The Congressman turned and smiled, "Well, not really, but you have to admit, we are winning over a better class of enemies!"

. . . .

Little Irving was reading about political intrigue in the weekly newspaper and turned to his father, "Dad, do political plums grow from seeds."

The old timer thought for a moment and replied, "Not really, they result from clever grafting."

. . . .

One day, with great fanfare, Radio Moscow announces that they have had such a surplus of flour this year that thousands of thousands of pounds of flour would be distributed free in front of one of the largest storehouses in Moscow. Soon, in freezing cold weather and in the wee hours of the morning, thousands begin to line up.

Five minutes before the appointed hour of distribution, a party official addresses the crowd via a loud speaker:

"All Jews on these lines must leave at once!"

Since all recipients of the flour would have to show identification papers, a great number turned away soulfully and walked off the lines.

About an hour later, another party officer goes to the loud speaker and declares:

"Are there any non-party members on line? If so, please leave at once!"

Three-quarters of those still on line, walk away, grumbling.

About two hours later, loyal communists still standing in the freezing rain, waiting for their free flour, see another party official mount the platform.

"Comrades," the speaker began, "We actually have no flour to distribute to anyone. In fact, we have no flour in all of Moscow — our crops this year were a total failure. However, the Bureau of Propaganda felt this would be an excellent device to carry abroad, that we have plenty of everything. I'm certain you will not mind having to waste a few hours whereby you have rendered your Party and country great service."

Most of the disappointed Communists began to disperse in silence, but one old timer shook his head sadly, "See, they accuse us of being unfair to the Jews, yet they always get preference and get to leave the line first!"

One of the lobbyists for the Federal Aid to Education bill spent the past three months trying to convince the members of Congress that such a bill was extremely important to the schools all over the country. One night, while asleep at home, his wife whispered, "Sam, wake up quick, there are burglars in the house!"

Sam, gave a snort, still very much asleep, and fell back asleep. His wife whispered a little louder, "Sam, there are burglars in the house!"

Sam, bleary eyed from a long day and a lack of sleep, muttered, "In the Senate, yes. In the House, no!"

. . . .

People who perform valuable services for the United Kingdom are honored annually with knighthood, bestowed by Her Majesty, Queen Elizabeth.

One year, an elderly British Jew was one of those honored for his outstanding contributions to his field of endeavor. Prior to being knighted, each honoree was required to recite a Latin phrase. For an entire month, this elderly Jew practiced saying his Latin phrase.

The big night came, and all the honorees stood in line to be knighted by the Queen. When it was the elderly Jew's turn to be knighted, his mind went blank. In desperation, he blurted out, *"Ma Nishtana Halayla Hazeh Mikol Haleilos."*

Thereupon Queen Elizabeth turned to her husband and asked, "Why is this knight different from all the other knights?"

Russia was having an election and all the peasants were urged to vote. On Election Day, one of the peasants entered the voting station and was handed a sealed envelope.

"Excuse me, sir," the peasant said to the armed guard, "What is this?"

The poll-watcher adjusted his rifle and said proudly, "This, comrade, is your Secret Ballot."

The peasant thanked the guard and began to open the envelope.

"What are you doing?" the guard shouted angrily.

"I want to see whom I'm voting for," the peasant exclaimed.

"Fool!" shouted the guard, "Don't you realize this is a *secret* ballot?"

. . . .

Sarah and her friend were in the supermarket shopping. To impress her friend with her worldly knowledge, Sarah asked, "Tell me, my dear, what do you think of Red China?"

Her friend smiled warmly and replied, "With a yellow tablecloth, it looks so nice!"

. . . .

The president of a local politics club was addressing the assembled membership, "In most organizations," he said, "Half the members do all the work, and the other half do nothing. I'm happy to say that in this club, we do the exact opposite!"

. . . .

The Russians claim that life in Russia is a paradise; they say each person has the same things. It so happened that at an important town meeting, the leading Commissar got up to speak to his people.

"And so to know how each of us has prospered, is there one among us who does not have an electric icebox and his own car?"

No one said a word. However, the hand of one of the listeners did go up. "Excuse me, comrade, but I do not have these things."

The Commissar looked down with dismay and shouted, "This is terrible! Sir, what is your name?"

"My name is Plotkin," exclaimed the citizen.

"Very well, Comrade Plotkin, we shall see that you get all these things. Guard, see that Comrade Plotkin gets everything that's coming to him."

Plotkin walked out with the guard.

A few days later, the Commissar was walking in the street and was stopped by one of the citizens who had been at the meeting.

"Comrade," exclaimed the citizen, "I just wanted to ask you about that fellow who said he didn't get all the glorious things you said we all have."

"Oh, yes, that was Plotkin. You want to know if he got his electric ice box and car, is that it?"

"Not quite, sir," he explained. "I just wanted to know what happened to Plotkin."

. . . .

To understand the American economy, you might ponder this little example:

A community built a new bridge. "Well," the residents said, "If we have a bridge, we had better have a watchman to keep an eye on things."

Then someone said, "Yes, but a watchman will need a salary."

So, they hired an accountant.

The accountant then explained that they would need a treasurer. With a watchman, an accountant and a treasurer, they had to have an administrator to direct them, so they appointed an administrator.

Then congress voted a reduction in funding and they had to cutback personnel. So they fired the watchman.

. . . .

Two Germans were fishing on a small stream that separated communist East Germany from the American zone of West Germany.

The West German was pulling in fish after fish. The East German was getting nothing.

After an hour of this, the East German called over, "Hey, how come you're pulling in so many fish and I can't even get a bite?"

The West German thought for a moment and then answered, "Maybe it's because the fish on this side aren't afraid to open their mouths!"

. . . .

Two politicians were arguing. One said, "You claim you're your own man. Well, what about the powerful interests that control every move you make and every cent you spend?"

The other politician stiffened and snapped, "Now wait a minute. I demand you leave my wife and my mother-in-law out of this!"

. . . .

When Winston Churchill came to America for a visit, he was only supposed to stay a few days visiting with American officials. However, he couldn't refuse the invitations from several famous American notables.

After canceling his first planned trip home, he wired his wife in London: "Am staying with the greatest Jewish Supreme Court Justice in this nation and one of the fine legal brains in this century, Justice Felix Frankfurter. He has invited me to his home for a week and I couldn't refuse."

The following week, he was invited to the home of Bernard Baruch. He wired his wife: "Am staying with the noted Jewish financier, Bernard Baruch, who has invited me to stay at his home a few days. The man is a genius."

The following week, he had accepted an invitation from Billy Rose, the great showman. Churchill wired his wife: "Am staying this week with Mr. Billy Rose, the great American showman of the Jewish faith. This man started from the lowest dregs of poverty and has now become one of the wealthiest Jews in the nation."

His wife wrote, "Well, when will you be home?"

Churchill cabled back, "*Noch Pesach!*" (after Passover)

Israel

Jewish dress manufacturer from New York got into the Israeli navy and was assigned the lookout post on a submarine. After he was in position, he noticed an enemy ship on the horizon. "Enemy cruiser sighted on the horizon," he shouted down to the captain. "Fire a torpedo."

The captain called back, "Good work, Schwartz, we have him in our sights."

A few minutes later, Schwartz called down, "The enemy cruiser is headed right in our direction. Please fire a torpedo."

The captain called back, "We are watching him."

A few minutes later, Schwartz shouted, "Enemy cruiser less than two hundred feet away! Please fire a torpedo! I'll pay for it!"

A jury in Israel went out to deliberate a case. After three long days of deliberation they filed back into the courtroom.

The judge asked, "Have you reached a verdict?"

The foreman got up and smiled, "Yes, your Honor."

"Please tell us your decision," the judge asked.

The foreman cleared his throat and declared, "We the jury have decided not to become involved."

. . . .

A little old lady from Brooklyn was flying to Israel and was seated next to a big Norwegian fellow who was staring out the window. In an effort to start a conversation, she asked softly, "Excuse me, please — but are you Jewish?"

The Norwegian fellow replied courteously, "No."

A few minutes later, the little old lady asked once more, "Listen, you're on a plane going to Israel, and who, after all, goes to Israel? So tell me, you're Jewish aren't you?"

The Norwegian, a little annoyed, turned to her and said, "Definitely not."

A few minutes later the little old lady asked once more, "Listen you don't have to be ashamed, most of us are Jewish. Tell me the truth, I know, I can tell you're Jewish. Are you Jewish?"

The Norwegian noticeably annoyed, and to get her to stop bugging him, snapped, "All right— so I'm Jewish!"

The little old lady looked at him and shook her head back and forth, "That's funny, you don't look Jewish at all."

A loud-mouthed Texan was visiting in Israel. As the guide took him around, he pointed to a new 20-story apartment complex and exclaimed, "Our people built that so fast, it took less than a year to complete!"

The Texan sneered, "Why, my friend, in Texas, a complex like that would go up in three months!" They moved along and came to a brand new power plant.

"Now, here is a new power station that took us less than three weeks to put up."

The Texan sneered once more, "Son, a building like that in Texas would probably take us a week to put up!"

Then they passed the new multi-story Diamond Center building, ablaze with lights. It truly was one of the most modern buildings in Israel.

"Say, son," asked the Texan, "What building is that across the street?"

The Israeli turned nonchalantly and replied, "I don't know, it wasn't there this morning."

. . . .

A military expert, commenting on the Israelis' swift invasion of Lebanon to clean out the PLO, which took just about six days, commented, "The Israelis had to move fast. They only rented the tanks for a week!"

A newspaper was sent a story about Israel and Egypt and the peace talks. It was a terrible liberal hatchet story. Enclosed with the manuscript was a note from the writer that said, "Please let me know immediately if you are going to use my story, since I have a number of irons in the fire."

The editor wrote back, "I am returning your story and advise you to put it with the other irons."

. . . .

A teacher asked her students, "If George Bush, Pat Buchanan and James Baker were in a sailboat and the sailboat turned over, who would get saved?" The answer was unanimous, "Israel!"

. . . .

A terrorist managed to creep through the border separating Israel from Lebanon, when suddenly there was a shot that went whistling right by his ear. Undaunted, the terrorist continued forward when another shot rang out and whistled through the turban on his head. He still pressed on.

Then a voice from the Israeli side called out, "One more step and I begin to take aim!"

. . . .

A Texan was talking to an Israeli farmer. The Texan began, "You know, in Texas, you can get in a car and drive around all day long — from sun up to sunset — and still remain on my farm!"

The Israeli smiled and replied, "Yes, I know. I once also had a car like that!"

· ·

A Texan, a Frenchman, and an Israeli were flying over the pacific when the plane's engines stopped functioning. The plane crashed and the three were immediately captured by a tribe of cannibals.

The chief told the three captives that since they were civilized, they had a custom that before they ate anyone, they granted that person a last wish. He asked the Texan, "What is your last wish?"

The Texan replied, "I want a two-inch high steak with all the trimmings, Cajun fries and a case of cold beer."

The Chief motioned to some of his tribesmen, who immediately ran into the jungle and came back with the food. The Texan ate his meal and was thrown into the pot.

The Frenchman was asked, "What is your last wish?" He replied, "I'd like a case of Dom Perignon and also a big plate of escargots cooked in the French manner."

The Chief motioned to his tribesmen, who immediately rushed off into the jungle and brought back everything the Frenchman asked for. He ate and drank his fill, and was then thrown into the pot.

The Chief turned to the Israeli and asked, "And what is your wish?" The Israeli looked the Chief squarely in the eyes and replied, "I would like you to kick me as hard as you can."

The Chief was bewildered, but followed his request. He asked the Israeli to turn around and kicked him as hard as he could. With that, the Israeli pulled out a gun and killed the Chief and all of the other cannibals.

The Texan and the Frenchman peeked out of the pot, looked at the Israeli and said, "If you had that gun, why didn't you do anything sooner?"

The Israeli replied, "And risk being condemned by the UN, EU, and the State Department for overreacting to insufficient provocation?"

* *

A visitor to Israel attended a recital and concert at the Moscowitz Auditorium. He was quite impressed with the architecture and the acoustics.

The visitor inquired of the tour guide, "Is this magnificent auditorium named after Chaim Moscowitz, the famous Talmudic scholar?"

"No," replied the guide.

"Is it named after Pascal Moscowitz, the renowned twentieth-century artist?"

"No," said the guide. "It is named after Sam Moscowitz, the writer."

"Never heard of him. What did he write?"

"A check!" replied the guide.

visitor to Israel recently commented to a native, "How come you use the same word for hello and goodbye?"

The Israeli smiled and declared, "With all our problems, half the time we don't know if we're coming or going..."

. . . .

wealthy Texan was visiting Israel. He had his luxurious Rolls Royce shipped to Israel so he could tour the country in comfort. One day while on the road, his car broke down and he called for a mechanic.

An Israeli mechanic drove up and raised the hood of the car, made a minor adjustment to the carburetor, closed the hood, and the car's motor turned over, humming like a top.

"How much do I owe you?" asked the Texan.

"That will be $50.05," the Israeli replied.

"Fifty dollars and five cents?" shouted the Texas. "And for just two seconds work? All you did was turn a little screw on the carburetor!"

The Israeli smiled warmly and replied, "I only charged you 5 cents for turning the screw, but I had to charge you $50 for knowing which screw to turn."

. . . .

wide-eyed tourist was being taken through the places of interest in the Land of Israel. Stopping at a cemetery, the tourist commented, "Oh, what a beautiful tomb! Whose is it?"

The guide, very straight-faced, replied, "That is the Tomb of the Unknown Soldier."

The tourist looked even more closely and spotted a name on the tombstone. "Just a minute...I can see a name on that stone. It says, 'Irving Hockmier.' I thought the unknown soldier did not have a name!"

"That's true," muttered the guide, regaining his composure. "As a soldier, Hockmier was unknown, but as a garment manufacturer, who didn't know him?"

. . . .

A young couple from Brooklyn visited Israel for vacation. As they sat on the shore looking out at the Mediterranean Sea, Sheldon, the young groom, waxed poetic. He leaned over the water and touched it gently with his hand.

"Roll on, thou deep and blue sea, roll on and on..." he said softly. His star-struck companion gazed out at the water for a moment then gushed excitedly, "Oh, Shlomo...it's listening! It's doing it!"

. . . .

A young man and his family had made *Aliyah* to Israel. After a few days, the young man found a very beautiful but expensive *Tallis* and decided to send it to his father in Brooklyn.

However, knowing his father was a rather frugal man, he had the merchant take off the $200 sticker that was attached to the *Tallis* and put on a price tag for $25. He shipped the

Tallis to his father and a few weeks later he got a letter back. It read, "My dear son Sheldon, thank you very much for the gorgeous *Tallis*. It was a good thing the merchant left the price tag in the package. See if you can pick up a few more. I was able to sell the one you sent for $30!"

• •

A young man from Texas was visiting Israel and was invited to dinner at the home of one of the local residents. As they sat down at the table, the Israeli took out a plate of huge black olives. The Texan had never seen olives and watched as the Israeli picked up an olive and began savoring its flavor.

The Texan gathered courage. He leaned over and picked up an olive. He put it in his mouth. The taste was strange and he couldn't spit it out into a napkin fast enough.

As the night wore on, the Israeli took olive after olive and savored the fruit. The Texan gathered courage once more and reached for another black olive. Once more the flavor was strange and he quickly spat it out.

The Israeli looked at him and smiled, "Don't you like olives?"

The Texan smiled uneasily and questioned, "Sure I do, but how can you tell which are the good ones?"

• •

An American businessman was visiting Israel. He asked a guide if there were any golf courses in Israel where he could keep trim.

"Golf..." exclaimed the guide, "...that's all we need! In a nation as tiny as ours, one good drive with a slight curve on the ball could create an international incident!"

. . . .

An American businessman met with the president of the United States a few days before he was to leave on his worldwide goodwill tour. Because of his diplomatic status, he was invited to the Oval Office in the White House, where the president was to thank him for his efforts.

As the businessman spoke with the president he noticed there were three phones on his desk — a red phone, a white phone and a blue phone.

"Excuse me, Mr. President," the business man said, "What are those three phones for?"

The president smiled and replied, "The red phone is a direct hot-line to the Kremlin. It is used in case of extreme emergency. The white phone I use for personal or business calls. And the blue phone," the president sighed, "that is a direct line to G-d."

The businessman asked if he could use the blue phone to seek G-d's blessings for his trip. The president handed him the phone and the man spoke into the phone for three minutes.

When he finished his call, he thanked the President and asked, "How much do I owe you for the call?"

The president sheepishly said, "That's $500, please."

The businessman handed the president a check for $500 and left for his world tour.

A few weeks later, he was in Israel and in the prime minister's office. There too, he saw three phones — a red, a white and a blue phone.

"What are they for?" the businessman asked innocently.

The Israeli Prime Minister replied, "The red phone is a hot-line direct to Washington for any emergencies. The white phone is for personal and business calls. And the blue phone is a direct line to G-d."

The businessman asked if he could use the blue phone to thank G-d for his safe trip. He was handed the phone and spoke again for three minutes.

When the call was finished he looked at the Prime Minister and asked, "How much do I owe you for the call?"

The Israeli Prime Minister smiled and said, "That'll be $1, please."

The businessman put his hand in his pocket and asked, "I don't understand. Why, just last month I used the blue phone in the office of President of the United States and the toll charge was $500. How come you only asked me for $1?"

The prime minister smiled warmly, "Because from here it's a local call!"

· ·

An American engineer was talking to an Israeli engineer. "Tell me," said the Israeli engineer, "When they build a tunnel in the United States, how do they do it?"

The American engineer declared, "Well, everything is exact.

We survey the land and feed the findings into a computer. This tells us the best place to begin. Then, we take a huge bulldozer that is connected to a computer. We begin digging and every inch of the way, the computer feeds out information and direction to the bulldozer on the other side of the tunnel — in fact, we measure again every inch of the way."

The American took a deep breath and asked, "Now, how do you build a tunnel in Israel?"

The Israeli engineer exclaimed, "Well, we take a fellow with a shovel, put him on one end of the bank and then we take a fellow with another shovel and put him on the other side. Then the two begin digging toward each other."

"My goodness," exclaimed the American engineer, "Don't you even take measurements for direction?"

"What measurements," exclaimed the Israeli, "The two fellows just dig toward each other."

"But what if they miss each other?" asked the American.

"Oh," exclaimed the Israeli, "In that case, we have two tunnels for the price of one!"

* *

An American general who, hearing of Israel's victory at war, called Israel's war-hero Moshe Dayan and asked his advice concerning the fighting in Vietnam.

Dayan allegedly wrote back, "Well, first it helps if you're fighting Arabs…"

An American industrialist, visiting Israel, was speaking to the head of a kibbutz. "It's amazing how quickly you people get things built here. Why, when I was here last year, that water line to irrigate the fields wasn't even up."

"Oh, that's nothing. We put up that line in less than a day," explained the Israeli.

"In less than a day?" gasped the American. "How could you have done it?"

"Simple," exclaimed the Israeli, "We get two of our youngest men to assemble the first two pieces of pipe to the pump, then we turn the water on and tell them to keep ahead of it!"

. . . .

An American newspaperman was interviewing an Israeli paratrooper. "Tell me," the reporter asked, "How many successful jumps have you made?"

The Israeli smiled innocently and exclaimed, "Every one of my jumps was successful. I'm here!"

. . . .

An American official had attended a rather special debate in which an Arab and an Israeli were discussing the merits of the Camp David Peace Accord.

The Arab representative got up to speak and spoke in a very clear English. He talked about the role the United States played and explained how the Arabs sought peace and how he felt the Camp David Accord was not the vehicle for peace.

The Israeli then got up to speak. He spoke only in Hebrew. At the end of his speech, the American official began to applaud.

An associate looked at the official and said, "Say, I didn't know you understood Hebrew?"

The American smiled and said, "I don't understand a single word of Hebrew."

"Then why are you applauding so vigorously?"

"Him," the American smiled warmly, "I trust!"

. . . .

An American tourist in Israel drove into an area where no parking was permitted. The driver approached a cop near the corner and asked, "Can I park here?"

The officer answered politely, in perfect English, "No."

"How come there are other cars parked here?" the tourist asked. "And if they can, why can't I?"

"They didn't ask me," he innocently replied.

. . . .

An American old timer went to Israel to tour the land. He stepped into one of the Israeli taxies and asked to be taken to some of the historic points of interest.

The driver took him to a variety of spots and as they were coming down one large mountain, suddenly the cab began to gain speed.

"Slow down, please," the American pleaded.

"I can't," shouted back the taxi driver, "The brakes are gone."

"Then for heaven's sake," shouted the American, "At least turn off the meter!"

. . . .

An American came to Israel to open a small brokerage office. In an effort to impress anyone who entered, he would pick up the phone and make believe he was talking to his broker all the way in New York.

One day, there was a knock on his office door. "Come in!" he shouted. Then, in an effort to impress the visitor, he picked up the phone, held it to his ear, and motioned to the visitor to sit down.

"I'll be with you in a minute," he said, then turned back to the phone and shouted, "Listen, when I deal with Merril Lynch, I expect results! Buy me 10,000 shares of the copper mine and 2,000 on the gold stock. Of course...also, the soy bean future, and I want my check for that sale of General Motors stock, okay? Goodbye."

He then smiled and turned to the visitor and asked, "Now, what can I do for you?"

The visitor rose a little uneasily and said, "I'm from the phone company. I came to hook up your phone..."

An American who was traveling through Israel suddenly realized he had left his hotel room without his wrist watch and he had to be in a certain village by 1:00pm.

As he drove along, he saw a farmer sitting by the road next to a cow. He pulled up, went over to the farmer and asked, "Excuse me, could you tell me what time it is?"

The farmer bent over toward the cow and took hold of the cow's tail. He then looked carefully for a few seconds and said, "The exact time is 12:34pm."

The man was amazed. He thanked the farmer and drove off. After he reached the village, he couldn't get over the way the farmer was able to tell time just looking at the bottom of the cow's tail.

On the way back from his meeting he saw the farmer once more. He stopped the car and went over to the farmer. "Excuse me, but you told me the time earlier today. Could you tell me what time it is now?"

The farmer leaned over again, reached for the cow's tail, and then said, "The exact time now is 5:43pm."

"I have never seen this before," the dumbfounded American exclaimed. "That is an amazing feat! How do you do it?" The farmer smiled and said that it wasn't anything unusual after all.

"Well, then," the American exclaimed. "Could you teach me how you do that?"

The farmer smiled and said, "Of course! Here, sit down next to me." The man sat down and waited. "Now," the farmer began once more, "Lean forward and hold the cow's tail."

The man followed the farmer's orders. "Now what?" he asked.

The farmer exclaimed, "Move the tail just a bit and if you look straight ahead you can see our town hall down the road with the clock on the outside...it's never wrong!"

. . . .

An Arab and an Israeli were discussing the archaeological finds of recent years.

"Do you know," exclaimed the Arab, "That a few weeks ago they discovered a piece of copper wire in the ancient sites just outside of Cairo?"

"*Nu*, so what does that prove?" questioned the Israeli.

"What does that prove? It proves that my ancestors, thousands of years ago, had the telegraph!" the Arab declared.

"How could you be so sure?" asked the Israeli.

"I'm sure!" smiled the Arab.

"Well, then," declared the Israeli, "While a group of my people were digging near the Western Wall last week, they did not discover any wire. Nothing! Not one strand!"

The Arab laughed, "So, what does that prove?"

The Israeli smiled and replied, "It proves that while your ancestors may have been busy with the telegraph, mine already went wireless!"

An Arab terrorist tried to take over a plane headed for Israel. "We will land in Cairo," the terrorist said, pointing a weapon at the pilot's head.

"We can't, with this size plane," explained the pilot. "We will have to lighten the load by a few hundred pounds at least."

The Arab ordered that all unnecessary equipment be tossed out the door. But despite the material tossed out of the plane, the pilot complained that the plane was still too heavy for a safe landing.

"We must lighten the load by a few hundred pounds more!"

"Okay," demanded the Arab, pointing the weapon at a French passenger, "You must jump!" The Frenchman rose to his feet proudly and walked to the door, took a deep breath and shouted, "*Vive La France!*" and jumped.

An Englishman was next. The Arab shouted, "Out!" The Britisher rose, walked to the door and shouted, "Long live the Queen!" and he jumped.

Then the Arab turned his weapon toward Isaac Shapiro and said, "You're next!"

Shapiro stood up proudly, walked toward the door and shouted, "*Shema Yisroel*," and pushed the Arab out the door.

• •

An Arab was being interviewed by an American correspondent. "I don't understand it," the correspondent began, "You had hundreds of thousands more men than Israel.

You had superior weapons. You had a superior air force, and yet Israel won the war."

"I blame it on the surprise attack," explained the Arab.

"What?" screamed the reporter, "With all your superior weapons?"

"Sure," explained the Arab, "That was the surprise!"

. . . .

An elderly woman got on an EL-AL airplane at Kennedy airport that was bound for Israel. She carried with her a small dog-carrier with a little dog inside. Once on the plane, she put the dog carrier on the seat next to her. When the stewardess saw this, she said, "Madam, I'm sorry we only allow guide dogs for blind people in the passenger section. Your dog will have to be placed in the luggage section."

The woman tearfully explained, "Listen, I bought an extra seat just for this purpose." They continued to argue. Finally, the captain came out and demanded the dog be put in the luggage bay of the plane.

When the plane arrived in Israel and the baggage carriers were unloading the luggage, they discovered the dog was dead. They all felt terrible. However, they decided to see if they could find a dog of the same breed, size and color to substitute for the dead one, hoping the old lady wouldn't notice. After scouring all of Israel, they finally found one and quickly replaced the dead dog with the live one. They then handed the old lady the little dog carrier.

She looked into the carrier and shouted, "*Gevald!* This is not my dog!"

The stewardess and the plane's captain kept trying to convince her that it was her dog and the dog was probably still excited from the trip. No matter what they said, she kept shouting, "This is not my dog!"

Finally, the plane captain asked, "What makes you so sure that isn't your dog?"

The little old lady sighed, "My dog was dead! I was taking it to be buried in Israel!"

. . . .

An Israeli citizen summed up the Kissinger policy of Israel returning the occupied territories in the Middle East. "You see, only a Jew could understand what they are doing. We call it the 'Salami Game.' Consider the occupied territories as a salami. They want us to shave off a little piece of salami at a time — never enough to really fight over. Finally, the victim is left with nothing but the string of the salami — and of course that's not enough to fight over, either!"

. . . .

An Israeli soldier on guard-duty spotted a Russian soldier, who was also on guard-duty on the other side of the Suez Canal.

The Israeli soldier jokingly called over, "Hey, Comrade, how are things in the Russian Army?"

The Russian called back, "Can't complain."

The Israeli called back, "You bet your sweet life you can't!"

. . . .

An old Jew was walking along the street in Jerusalem when he was stopped and assaulted by an Arab. As the old timer picked himself up off the ground, he handed the Arab a shekel. "Thank you so much for hitting me!" the old Jew declared to the surprise of the Arab.

"You see," continued the old man, "Today is a special kind of Jewish holiday, in which it is a great blessing for a Jew to be hit by an Arab. And according to the holiday, when this happens, the Jew is supposed to give a reward to the person who punches him. Since I am a poor man, all I can afford is a shekel. However, since you were so kind to help me out, I want to tell you to go to that house across the street where another Jew lives. I believe he also observes this holiday. If you wait until he comes out and you really give it to him, I am certain he will reward you much better than I have."

The Arab thanked the old timer and waited in front of the house. In a few minutes the man walked out. The Arab approached him and unleashed a barrage of punches.

The man, a former prize-fighter and good friend of the old Jew, let loose with a few professional hooks of his own and totally flattened the Arab. He then walked away without saying a word.

When the Arab woke up, he scratched his head in surprise

while musing, "Just my luck to run into one of those Jews who doesn't observe this holiday!"

* *

An old lady delivered a letter to the post office, the clerk weighed the letter and said, "Lady, this letter weighs more than an ounce. You will have to put another stamp on it."

The old woman snapped back, "Is that so? And if it would have weighed less than an ounce would you have refunded me the difference?"

* *

An old timer walked into a bank in Israel and asked, "How much would you charge me for a $25 loan?"

The manager of the loan office said, "We have a minimum interest of $5 that is charged on loans. Besides, you also have to have some collateral."

"Could I put my car up for the collateral?" the old timer asked.

The loan manager smiled, "That really wouldn't be necessary for such a small loan. On major loans, we require a car for collateral and we have to keep the car in our company garage until the loan is paid off."

"I don't want any special favors," the old timer exclaimed, "I would worry that someone might steal the car, or worse yet, get into an accident and I would be left without a collateral.

I insist that you keep the car in your bank's garage until the loan is paid off."

The manager realized the old man was sincere, so he said, "Okay, just bring in the car and when your loan is paid off, you'll get the car back. How's that?"

The old timer was satisfied. The following day, he brought his car to the garage. As he left, the attendant said, "You're kind of silly to leave a car here all winter for a measly $25 loan."

The old timer smiled. "Listen, now that winter has started, I'm going on vacation to the hot springs for several weeks. Where else could I park my car in a heated garage for that length of time for only the $5 interest on the loan?"

. . . .

Cohen was visiting relatives in Israel when suddenly a band of Arab guerrillas began firing missiles at the tiny kibbutz he was staying at. As he and his wife started running for the shelter, he stopped in the middle of the field.

"Wait, wait!" he shouted to his wife, "I have to run back."

"Run back?" screamed his wife, "Why?"

"I forgot my teeth! I left them in the bathroom in a glass."

"Forget your teeth!" his wife screamed, "What do you think they are firing at us? Salami sandwiches?"

During WWI and WWII, the United States Army distributed K-Rations to their soldiers. It was basic survival food and not very tasty.

In Israel, an Israeli military man was explaining to an American general, "We also have a system of K-Rations, only in Israel, K-Rations has a different meaning. For example, our K-Rations are *Katchkeh*, *Knishes*, *K'replach*, *K'naidlach*, *Kishkeh*, *Kasha* and *Kugel*."

The American general was amazed. "And what do they have for dessert?"

The Israeli soldier replied with pride, "*Kichel!*"

. . . .

Harriette called the British Embassy and shouted into the phone, "Hello? Hello?"

"Yes, can I help you?" a very British speaking young lady asked.

"I want to speak to the Ambassador to complain about what he's doing to Israel."

"I'm sorry," the young lady cut in, "But the Ambassador has gone to the United Kingdom."

"Oh, I'm sorry," sighed Harriette, "When was the funeral?"

. . . .

In the last moments of the war, one of the remaining battalions of Egyptians left fighting in the desert, spotted an Israeli soldier darting behind a sand dune. The Egyptian commander sent three of his top men to wipe out the resistance.

Ten minutes passed and the three Egyptians did not return. The commander, angered, sent ten more men to find out what was causing the delay. He waited half an hour, and, once more, none of the men returned. In a rage, he ordered the entire company to proceed to the sand dune to wipe out the Israeli soldier.

In a few minutes, there was a terrible racket and almost the entire company was wiped out. But, somehow, one Egyptian soldier managed to return to the commander.

"What happened?" the commander shouted, "I sent the whole company in to wipe out one Israeli!" The soldier breathing his last, sighed, "You were wrong, sir - there wasn't one Israeli back there — there were two!"

· ·

It could only happen in Israel. Moshe Dayan was near the front lines and was turning the corner of a building when a young Israeli private came tearing around the building in a hurry and collided with him.

"Here! Here!" Dayan said, pulling himself back together, "Do you know who I am?"

The young Israeli soldier snapped, "I suppose you're gonna tell me you're our great general, Moshe Dayan?"

"Exactly," replied Dayan.

"Oh, yeah," snapped the young Israeli, "Well, General, do you know who I am?"

Dayan looked concerned and said, "No — who?"

"Thank G-d!" snapped the G.I. as he fled off into the darkness.

. . . .

Mama and Papa were sending a package to their son in Israel. When they got to the post office the clerk weighed the package and exclaimed, "It's too heavy — you'll have to put more stamps on it."

Papa smiled and questioned, "*Nu*, if we put more stamps on it, that will make it lighter?"

. . . .

Once aboard an EL AL plane, the stewardess welcomed all the passengers over the loud speaker system:

"Good afternoon, ladies and gentlemen. I hope you have a lovely trip to Israel. Let me introduce myself — I am your stewardess, Mrs. Rose Bergman, and of course, my son, Sol, is the pilot."

. . . .

Since Israel wrapped up their military obligations with the Arabs in six days, it was rumored that an Israeli general notified President Johnson that Israel would consider taking over the Vietnam war for cost plus 10%!

ISRAEL

Some years ago, when David Ben Gurion was resigning for the ninth time as the prime minister of Israel, an American reporter asked him if this meant he was retiring from politics.

Ben Gurion smiled warmly and explained, "Not at all. Listen...my resigning has the same significance as those "Going Out Of Business" signs along Seventh Avenue in New York City. Like me — those businessmen get a chance to unload some stock they don't want, hire new men, and make a different contract with the union!"

. . . .

Somebody finally figured out how an American could make a small fortune in Israel.

You come with a large one!

. . . .

The Israeli Navy was involved in fleet maneuvers and the admiral in charge of naval operations nearly burst a blood vessel when he bumped his vessel into a nearby ship, after which both were locked together. The ship was commanded by a young naval officer who started to tremble.

The admiral, not certain what maneuver the young officer was going to make to untangle the ships, yelled, "What do you intend to do now?"

The young officer flashed back, "Buy a small farm near a kibbutz, Sir!"

The Israeli police department is probably the best in the world, so when the New York police sent them four photographs of a most wanted criminal — a front view, left side view, back view and right profile — the Israeli police wired back in less than twenty-four hours. "Got your photographs and are holding all four men in custody to await your orders!"

. . . .

The Israeli who came to America was terribly confused. "I don't understand you Americans. First you make hot tea, then put ice in it to make it cold. Then you put sugar in it to make it sweet, then squeeze in lemon to make it sour. Then you lift the glass and say, 'Here's to you!' and drink it yourself!"

. . . .

There was one old timer who used to sit in the same spot everyday in front of a tourist hotel. The bellhops used to tell the tourists that this man was so nuts that when anybody would hold up a quarter and a $5 bill, permitting him to make a choice, the old timer would smile and choose the quarter. Day after day tourists would giggle at the simple old timer.

One day, when nobody was around, a visitor engaged the old man in conversation. "Don't you know that a $5 bill is worth much more than a quarter?"

The old timer smiled warmly and, with a twinkle said, "Of course I do, but the minute I accept a $5 bill, I'm out of business. I'm no simpleton. I've been here for six years now, earning a nice living for my family from all the quarters the people give me!"

· ·

Three old timers were sitting on a bench in one of those small parks in Brooklyn. Hymie exclaimed, "I was just thinking, what's a good definition for the word 'fame?'"

"*Nu*," exclaimed Abe, "So what would you call the word 'fame?'"

"To me," exclaimed Hymie, "Fame would be if I should go to Israel and have David Ben Gurion invite me over to his house for supper."

"*Neh*," snapped Abe, "To me, fame would be being invited to Ben Gurion's house for dinner and when his phone rings, he lets it ring because he enjoys my conversation more."

Shmuel, listening to the conversation, didn't say a word.

"*Nu*" asked Hymie and Abe, "What would you consider fame, Shmuel?"

Shmuel smiled for a moment, then exclaimed, "Fame to me would be like you said, going to Israel and having Ben Gurion invite you over for supper and then the phone rings. But, Ben Gurion answers the phone, listens for a minute, then hands me the phone and says, 'Shmuel it's for you!' That's fame!"

Two Americans, who had made *Aliyah* to Israel, were talking, "And did you hear, my neighbor's son is in the navy!"

The second questioned, "On which ship?"

The first replied, "You mean we got more than one?"

. . . .

Two characters from New York met in Israel. One was very thin; the other quite fat. The fat one giggled, "You know, Meyer, when the Israelis take one look at you, they'll think we have famine in America!"

Meyer countered, "And when they take one look at you, they'll swear you caused it!"

. . . .

When Levi Eshkol was here, he met with all the local dignitaries at City Hall. Meeting one high official, Eshkol shook his hand. The official proudly exclaimed, "Mr. Eshkol, I want you to know that I am an American first, a government official second and a Jew last!"

Eshkol smiled knowingly and is alleged to have commented, "So, what have you got to worry about? If anything ever goes wrong, in Israel, we read from right to left!"

Doctors & Medicine

. . . .

A doctor met one of his patients on the street. "I'm glad to see you looking so fit, Mrs. Goldberg," the doctor exclaimed. "Oh, by the way, I'm sorry to mention it, but your check came back."

The woman looked at the doctor and sighed, "So did my arthritis!"

. . . .

A fellow walked into a doctor's office for an examination. When the doctor finished and diagnosed the case, he wrote out a prescription and handed it to the patient. When the patient was ready to leave, he handed the doctor $2.

"I beg your pardon, Mr. Shapiro," the doctor exclaimed, "My fee is $10, not $2."

"That's news to me," exclaimed Shapiro, "My neighbor said it was only $5!"

. . . .

A little old lady was walking down the street when she met her doctor. "How are you, Mrs. Goldberg?" the doctor said cordially.

"Oy," sighed Mrs. Goldberg, "Not well. Not well at all!"

"Then why don't you stop by my office," the doctor replied.

Mrs. Goldberg smiled sweetly and replied, "Thank you, doctor, I will as soon as I feel a little better."

. . . .

A man and his wife entered a dentist's office on the Lower East Side. "Please, I want to have a tooth pulled," exclaimed the woman. "And don't bother with Novocain or Twilight gas."

"Well," said the dentist, "It's a little irregular. You sure are brave. Which tooth is it, madam?"

"Irving," exclaimed the woman, "Quick, show the dentist your tooth."

A man goes to his doctor and complains of a backache. "Well, I'm going to try a new treatment on you," the doctor exclaimed. "All you have to do is go home and say, as many times as possible, 'Every day, in every way, I feel better and better.' This, I'm sure, will work."

The patient went home and a week later he returned.

"Well," asked the doctor, "What happened?"

"It was like you said," began the patient, "I went home and said 100 times, 'Every day, in every way, I feel better and better.'"

"*Nu?*" exclaimed the doctor.

"To tell the truth, I actually felt better every day in every way, but at night, *Oy vey!*...did I feel sick!"

. . . .

A man was obsessed with the idea that he had a cat inside his head. *Nu? A mishugas!* All attempts to convince him that there was no cat wandering around in his head had failed. A psychiatrist realized that a teacher once told him as a child that he had *ah kahtz in kup*, and so the thought stuck with him.

In an attempt to cure him of this terrible obsession, the doctor was forced to perform a mock operation. All the necessary preparations were made. An operating room was reserved, they marked his head with medicines and, after the man was given an anesthetic, his head was wrapped in bandages.

Before the patient came to the doctor, he had already prepared the scene with a dead black cat.

"You were right," the doctor beamed, "You did have a cat wandering around in your head. And here it is!" The doctor held up the black cat for the patient to see. But, Goldberg turned woefully away and began to sob.

"What's the trouble, Mr. Goldberg?" the doctor questioned.

The man tearfully exclaimed, "That isn't mine! The cat in my head is gray!"

· ·

A patient complained to his doctor, "Doctor, my wooden leg is causing me pain." The doctor laughed, "How could a wooden leg cause you pain?"

The patient replied, "My business partner hits me over the head with it!"

· ·

A patient walked into his doctor's office and exclaimed, "Doctor, I need your help. I seem to be forgetting everything. I can't remember from one minute to the other. What should I do?"

"Well," exclaimed the doctor, "Considering your condition, the first thing you must do is pay me in advance."

A sweet little old lady walked into a chiropractor's office. The old woman was practically bent in half; her body was so bent over she could hardly walk. She supported herself from falling over with a tiny cane that was maybe six inches long.

When the chiropractor took one look at her, he turned to his other patients in the waiting room and said, "I hope you can excuse me. This looks like an emergency. This woman needs help. Look how she's bent over!"

He ushered the old lady straight into his office. Ten minutes later, the door opened and the woman walked out as straight as a board. She was now supporting herself with a full-sized cane and walking upright.

The patients in the office were amazed. "Look," said one of them, "This doctor must be a miracle man. She walked in bent over, almost to the floor, leaning on a tiny six-inch cane. Now look at her — she's as straight as a board, walking practically upright!"

The old lady turned and snapped, "He's no miracle man! All he did was give me a longer cane."

· ·

A wealthy man walked into a doctor's office. The doctor kept looking at him and after a while, the man asked the doctor, "What is it doctor? Why are you looking at me in that way?"

The doctor sighed, "I'm trying to figure out what kind of disease you could afford."

A woman had a broken pipe in her basement and called a plumber. The plumber arrived and in fifteen minutes replaced the pipe. He then handed her a bill for $150."

"What?" exclaimed the woman. "Why, my doctor comes to the house to treat my husband and four children and the most he's ever charged was $50."

The plumber sighed and nodded, "I know. That's what I used to charge when I was a doctor!"

. . . .

A woman wasn't feeling well, so she went to her doctor. "Doctor, I don't understand it, I just don't feel like eating anymore."

The doctor examined her and explained, "Look, your whole system is run down. By not eating, you are destroying yourself. Here, take these pills. They will stimulate an appetite. Don't eat anything until you have an appetite."

The woman left and made an appointment for the following week. When she returned, the doctor asked her, "Well, how do you feel?"

"Your pills didn't work," she said softly. "I didn't have an appetite all week."

The doctor gasped, "You mean to tell me you haven't eaten all week?"

The woman shrugged her shoulders, "Not quite. You see, I waited and waited until I got an appetite, but I never got one."

"What did you do for nourishment?"

"What?" the woman shrugged, "I ate when I got hungry!"

. . . .

A young doctor was called to treat an old gentleman. The doctor examined his patient and then wrote out a prescription. "Have this prescription filled," the doctor exclaimed, "In a few days, you should feel much better."

As the doctor prepared to walk out he noticed how poverty stricken the family was. He stopped for a moment, took out a $50 bill from his pocket and left it on the kitchen table. A few days later, the doctor called up to see how the old man was.

"*Oy*, doctor, G-d should bless you," the old timer exclaimed. "The money you left on the kitchen table was so generous of you. And *takeh*, like you said, I feel wonderful."

The doctor was very pleased. "*Nu*, so tell me...what did you do with the money?" the doctor asked.

"I went to a specialist and now I'm all better," the old man replied.

. . . .

A young doctor was talking to an old timer who had been practicing medicine for years. "I admire you tremendously; how you can keep your wits about you listening to your patient's complaints all day long?"

The old timer smiled, "Who listens?"

A young intern was asked to take over for the old time doctor who was called away on an emergency. In walked a man looking very weak and gaunt, his skin was terrible — it was almost impossible to diagnose him.

The young intern ran into the doctor's inner office, opened the medical books, but could find nothing to fit the description of the patient. But he knew he had to say something, so he returned to the examining room and asked, "Have you ever had this before?"

The man said, "Why yes!"

The intern sighed, "Well, I'm afraid you got it again!"

· ·

A young man walked into a therapist's office and says to the doctor, "Doc, I've lost all desire to go on. Life is just too fast and too hectic."

The psychiatrist says, "That's understandable. We all have problems. You'll need a number of years of treatment and I charge $175 an hour."

The young man thought for a few moments, looked at the psychiatrist and said, "Well, that solves your problems, Doc. Now, what about mine?"

· ·

A young man walked into the office of a very successful doctor who had sort of a medical assembly line for his patients. The harried nurse at the reception desk motioned for him to go into the next room and simply said, "Go in there! The doctor will be with you in a few minutes."

The young man replied, "Wait...wait..."

The nurse snapped, "Please, don't argue with me! Get into the next room and the assistant will help you. Tell your problems directly to the doctor."

The young man dutifully went into the next room and was met by a brawny orderly, who snapped, "Change into this robe, while I step out."

The young man pleaded, "Please, listen..."

The orderly shouted, "Haven't got time. Just get into this robe and the doctor will be with you shortly."

In a few minutes the doctor arrived, put the young man on the examining table, checked his heart, his lungs and blood pressure. The doctor looked up and said, "My friend, you are the picture of health. Why did you come to see me?"

The young man turned with disgust and replied, "I just came to read your electric meter!"

. . . .

A young man walks into a psychiatrist's office. "Doctor," the young man exclaimed, "I find that I am talking to myself."

The doctor tried to comfort him, "That's not so bad. A great many people talk to themselves."

The young man sighed, "That may be true, but you don't know what a *nudnik* I am!"

A young man was walking down the street when he sees his doctor walking out of a store. He runs over and says, "Hey, six weeks ago, when I was in your office with a terrible cough, you said I should go home, get into bed and stay there until you called. But you never called!"

"I didn't?" the doctor questioned, "Then, what are you doing out of bed?"

. . . .

According to the most recent psychiatric journal, psychiatrists claim that three out of every four Americans may be mentally ill. So, if three of your friends seem normal, *Gevald,* are you in trouble!

. . . .

An elderly lady from Brooklyn was a terrible hypochondriac who called her doctor every night, at all hours, to complain about imaginary aches and pains.

In exasperation, the doctor shouted over the phone, "Mrs. Rosenberg, if you wake me once more in the middle of the night with those crazy stories about something bothering you, I'm going to have to ask you to find another doctor. A doctor is to be called only when a person is really sick, but you are as healthy as can be!"

A few days later, the old lady accidentally fell down some stairs, breaking her leg, four ribs and suffering a concussion as well. The doctor was called and examined her from head to toe. Then he stood back, shook his head approvingly and

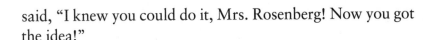

said, "I knew you could do it, Mrs. Rosenberg! Now you got the idea!"

. . . .

An Irishman, Scotsman, and a Jewish businessmen were partners. All three were getting on in years and were beginning to get various aches and pains. Each complained of the same symptoms. It was decided that one would go to the doctor and whatever medicine the doctor prescribed, the three would take the same medicine. It was also agreed that they would share the doctor's bill to save on the fee. So, the Irishman was selected to go.

The following afternoon, he came back with a very sad look on his face. "Gentlemen, we have only six months to live!"

They all gasped.

Finally, the Irishman declared, "Well, I'm not going to waste those months. I'm going back to old Ireland to enjoy my last moments."

The Scotsman chimed in, "And I'm going back to Scotland where I can likewise enjoy my last days."

They turned to the Jewish partner and asked, "And what are you going to do, Sam?"

The old timer smiled uneasily and explained, "I'm going to see a specialist!"

An old timer came running into his doctor's office and exclaimed, "Doctor! Doctor, help me! I have a dime stuck in my ear!"

"How long has it been stuck in your ear?" the doctor questioned, examining the patient's ear.

"About two weeks," the man answered.

"Two weeks?" the doctor gasped. "Why did you wait so long?"

The old timer smiled sheepishly and exclaimed, "To tell you the truth, I didn't need the money till now."

. . . .

An old timer went to his doctor. After the examination, the doctor said, "Mr. Cohen, if I said an operation would be necessary, would you be able to afford it?"

The old timer smiled and replied, "And if I couldn't afford it, doctor, the operation wouldn't be necessary?"

. . . .

An old timer went to his doctor. The doctor examined his patient and then said, "My friend, you are a very sick man. You should be hospitalized immediately. Is there anyone you want me to call?"

The old timer sighed, "Yes...another doctor!"

An old woman goes to her doctor and complains "Doctor, you have to help me! It hurts me here," she pointed with her finger to her shoulder.

Then she added, "...and it hurts me here," pointing with her finger to her stomach. "And it hurts me here," she exclaimed once more, pointing to her knee. "Tell me, doctor, what is it?"

The doctor replied, "Personally, I think you have a broken finger."

· ·

Cohen had been in the catering business for years, but when business got bad he was forced into bankruptcy and took a job in an office. The only problem was he couldn't get up on time to get into the office.

"Listen, Cohen," exclaimed his boss, "Why don't you see a doctor? The fact that you can't sleep at night and then come in late to work is hurting your efficiency and I will not stand for it too much longer."

Cohen took his advice. He went to his doctor who gave him some sleeping pills. That night he went to bed and fell asleep immediately and had a pleasant rest. In the morning, the alarm rang. He jumped out of bed full of vim and vigor and arrived at the office bright and early and greeted his boss.

"Say, you know, that was the best advice anyone has ever given me. Going to my doctor for sleeping pills really worked. I had no trouble getting up this morning."

The boss sighed, "That's nice, but where were you yesterday?"

Cohen happened to sit at the same table as Doctor Finkelstein during a summer's weekend. All through the meal, day in and day out, Cohen fired questions at the doctor concerning his aches and pains. Finally, in disgust, the doctor sent a bill to Cohen for professional services rendered.

In anger, Cohen called his lawyer and asked, "Am I legally bound to pay him?"

The lawyer said, "Yes you are," and then sent Cohen a bill for legal advice.

. . . .

Cohen meets a friend on the street and says, "I'm getting so forgetful lately." His friend asks, "So why don't you go to a doctor?"

The friend says, "I did."

The other fellow asks, "*Nu*, so what happened?"

Cohen shrugged his shoulders and sighed, "I forgot what he said!"

. . . .

Cohen was sitting on a bench in the park when his old friend wandered by. "*Nu*, Chaim, how's the arthritis?" the first fellow questioned.

"Thank G-d, much better! *Oy* did I find a doctor! He's so wonderful!"

"Amazing!" gasped his friends. "I've been suffering for years with arthritis and still can't find a decent doctor. How is this doctor so wonderful?"

"How?" laughed Cohen, "When I went to him, I told him that every time I raise my arm I get terrible pains."

"*Nu*, so what did he prescribe?" asked his friend.

"Nothing, he said I shouldn't raise my arm that way, and from that day on, no pains, no nothing!"

. . . .

Cohen was talking to his partner. "*Oy*, have I got a son. He's only out of medical school one year and already he's discovered a cure for which there's no disease!"

. . . .

Cohen wasn't feeling too well, so he went to a doctor. The doctor told him he had to stop drinking whiskey immediately. When he came home, his wife asked, "So, what did the doctor say?"

"He said I have to stop drinking whiskey immediately."

"So why are you having a glass of whiskey right now?" she asked.

Cohen replied, "I'm making believe I'm going to see the doctor tomorrow instead of today."

. . . .

Cohen would purchase a lottery ticket every chance he could. Finally, one day, while he was in the park, the phone rang in his home. His wife picked up the phone and heard it was the lottery commission, who told her that her husband had just won $100,000! Realizing her husband had a bad heart, she quickly called her doctor and asked his advice.

"First, let me congratulate you. Second, tell him I want him to stop by my office tomorrow for his annual checkup. While he's here, I'll break the news to him gently. And if anything goes wrong, I'll be here to minister to him. But I'm certain nothing will happen!"

The following day, Cohen went to his doctor and, as he was being examined, the doctor made idle conversation.

"So what do you do in your spare time?" the doctor asked.

"What do I do?" Cohen replied, "Listen, when you're seventy years of age, what is there to do? I walk in the park and I buy a lottery ticket every so often."

The doctor smiled and said, "*Nu,* so tell me...what would you do if you *takeh* won the $100,000 lottery prize?"

Cohen smiled back, put his hand on the doctor's shoulder and sighed, "Doctor, if I won the $100,000 lottery, I'd give half to you!"

With that, the doctor fainted.

. . . .

C ome, come, Mrs. Liebowitz," exclaimed the doctor, "Now we'll find out what makes you tick!"

"Please doctor, I don't care about what makes me tick. But

tell me, what is it that makes me chime every quarter of an hour?"

. . . .

David Breger, the accountant, called the doctor one night and excitedly exclaimed, "Doctor, come quick, my wife just accidentally swallowed my fountain pen!"

The doctor said he would rush right over, concluding with, "What are you doing in the meantime?"

Breger answered, "I'm using a pencil!"

. . . .

During a routine exam, an old timer looked up and said, "Doctor, I want you to give me something to invigorate me. I want something to stir me up to get back in fighting trim. Do you have a prescription like that for me?"

The doctor smiled warmly and replied, "Yes. My bill!"

. . . .

Fogelman walked into a therapist's office and sighed, "Please...help me!"

The therapist asked him to sit down. "Now, tell me your problem."

"I own a summer home in the mountains and a home in Plainview. My son just got a brand new yacht, and my wife got a fancy mink coat and a brand new Cadillac."

"That's wonderful," exclaimed the therapist. "So tell me, what is your problem?"

Fogelman sighed, "But I only make fifty dollars a week!"

. . . .

Goldberg ran to his doctor and exclaimed, "Doctor, I think I'm losing my mind. My memory is almost gone. No sooner do I say something then I forget what I said."

"How long has this been going on?" asked the doctor.

"How long has what been going on?" questioned Goldberg.

. . . .

Goldberg went to the doctor for an examination. He wasn't feeling too well. After the examination, the doctor said, "Mr. Goldberg, all your tests came out perfect. You are in perfect health. Your illnesses are all in your imagination. You have an excellent constitution. As a matter of fact, you will probably outlive me!"

Goldberg turned to the doctor and sighed, "Doctor, you're just saying that to make me feel good."

. . . .

Herbert Cohen called his doctor because he had a terrible headache. The telephone answering service answered the phone and Cohen asked to speak with the doctor.

"I'm sorry," the operator exclaimed, "the doctor is out for

the evening. However, if you tell me what's wrong, maybe I can help you."

Cohen explained that he had a splitting headache.

"Oh," exclaimed the operator, "Why don't you take a little schnapps and tea and go to bed. Then call the doctor in the morning."

The following morning, Cohen called the doctor as he was directed to do. The same operator at the answering service answered the phone. He told her he still didn't feel too well.

"The doctor isn't in yet," she exclaimed, "Why don't you take two aspirins and try calling him back a little later this evening."

Cohen waited a few hours, then, when the pain became intense, he dialed the doctor's number once more and the doctor himself picked up the phone.

"Can I help you," the doctor asked.

Cohen, cleared his throat and hesitatingly exclaimed, "If you don't mind, I'd rather talk to your operator, she's familiar with my case!"

. . . .

It was 3:00am when the doctor's phone rang. "Hello, doctor," a voice shouted over the phone. "I don't feel well and I want you to come to my house as soon as possible!"

The doctor replied, "I don't make house calls anymore; however, if it is an emergency, I could come, but I will have to charge you $50 for the house call."

"How much do you get for an office visit?" the caller asked.

"I get $20 for an office visit," the doctor replied.

"Okay," replied the caller, "I'll meet you in your office in ten minutes!"

. . . .

Louie was called out on an ambulance emergency. He leaned over the accident victim and asked, "Are you comfortable?"

The old-timer looked up and replied softly, "Thank G-d, I make a living!"

. . . .

Moishe asked his friend, "*Nu*, so how's your wife?"

"Not so good. She's suffering from acute *Frontal Sinusitis*," Abe explained.

"Oh my goodness!" Sam declared, "Where did she get that from?"

"From a radio commercial yesterday!" Moishe sighed.

. . . .

One old timer went to his doctor. After the examination, the old timer asked, "*Nu*, doctor, so what's wrong with me?"

The doctor scratched his head as he checked the records,

then replied, "I really don't know. I'm trying to figure out something you can afford."

. . . .

Rabinowitz wasn't feeling too well and a friend suggested they go to a doctor. When they reached the doctor's office, Rabinowitz took one look at the sign on the door and exclaimed, "I'm not going in!"

"Why? All of a sudden you became healthy?" his friend quipped.

"No, no, I still feel terrible. But look at the sign on this doctor's door!"

The friend read the sign aloud, "It says, 'Dr. Schwartz 9 to 1' — what's wrong?"

"Listen," sighed Rabinowitz, "With odds like that I don't stand a chance!"

. . . .

Sadie was just being wheeled out of the operating room and back to her room. Once she was settled in bed she sighed, "Thank G-d that's over!"

"Don't be so sure," the patient in the next bed exclaimed. "They operated on me last week and then had to open me up again because they left a sponge inside."

The patient in the next bed sighed, "And Sadie, let me tell you...when they operated on me two weeks ago, they

had to open me up again because the doctor left one of the instruments inside."

Just then Sadie's doctor stuck his head into the room and called out, "Excuse me ladies, has anyone here seen my hat?"

Sadie fainted.

· ·

S adie Yachenflaster walked into her dentist's office and exclaimed, "*Oy*, have I got a toothache. *Oy*, doctor, have I got a toothache!"

The dentist worked on the tooth and in a few minutes the pain had subsided. "Now, when you go home," he explained, "There may be a little swelling. If that happens, put an icepack on your cheek."

Sadie listened intently then asked, "A cold ice pack or a hot ice pack?"

· ·

T he door to the waiting room opened and in walked a young lady. "Doctor, doctor, I came here to find out what's wrong with me," she exclaimed.

The doctor looked at her and said, "Well, I don't even have to do an examination. I can tell exactly what's wrong with you. First, you don't eat enough. Second, you use too much makeup, and third, there is definitely something wrong with your eyes!"

"How could you tell that?" the girl questioned.

"Well, for one thing, my sign outside says 'Veterinarian!'"

The specialist, after writing out a prescription, said to Solomon Gisswasser, "My fee is $25."

Gisswasser, a character from the East Side commented, "That's too much."

"Then give me what you can afford," replied the doctor in exasperation.

"I can't give you anything." Gisswasser replied.

"Then why did you come to me? You know I'm very expensive. Why didn't you go to a clinic?"

Gisswasser smiled weakly and replied, "When it comes to my health — money is no object!"

. . . .

There's a wonderful story told about a young doctor who attended a sick child and managed to pull the youngster through a severe crisis. A few days later, the grateful father stopped in at the doctor's office and, after expressing the fact that no money in this world could repay him for the service he performed, added, "But I hope you will accept this little hand-tooled leather wallet I made especially for you in my home workshop; it was made with love and eternal gratitude."

The doctor very coldly exclaimed, "Gifts maintain friendships, but money maintains a family."

The man was taken back and said, "I'm sorry; what is your fee?"

The doctor replied, "$200."

The man took back the wallet, opened it, took from it five

$100 bills, withdrew two $100 bills, handed it to the doctor, and left.

. . . .

Two fellows were in a hospital ward, both suffering from an injured ankle. A young intern entered the room, walked over to the first fellow and began examining his injury. The intern pulled and twisted the ankle with an impressive air. With every twist and turn, the patient howled with pain.

Then the intern turned to the second patient and went through the same pulling and stretching of the ankle, but the poor fellow in bed didn't utter a sound.

After the doctor left, the fellow in the first bed said, "Gee, I admire you. How were you able to withstand all that pain?"

The second fellow sighed, "As a matter of fact, I can't stand pain. I just used common sense!"

"What do you mean, common sense?" the first patient asked.

The second patient smiled, "Do you think I was crazy enough to show him my injured ankle?"

. . . .

Yankel met a friend who was all excited. "Yankel," the friend began, "You know, I have been having trouble with my hearing. So I went to this place and for $1,000 they fitted me with a hearing device that is the best in the world. I can hear the sound of a fly at twenty paces. This device is incredible."

Yankel asked, "What kind is it?"

His friend smiled and replied, "A quarter past two!"

. . . .

Zelda Tzukreinken, a hypochondriac of the first order, always complained about something being wrong with her. Finally, one day, she went to a doctor who had been alerted that the woman was as healthy as could be, but that she had to be humored for her imaginary illness. Finally, after the examination, she exclaimed weakly, "*Nu,* doctor, how do I stand?"

The doctor thought for a moment and muttered, "I really don't know. To me it's a miracle!"

"You're an angel," she purred and left a happy woman.

Old Age

. . . .

A little old lady was riding on a subway and spoke to a young man next to her, *"Kenst reden yiddish?"* (Can you speak Yiddish?)

The young man shook his head, signifying that he did not understand her. She looked so flustered. Then she turned to another man seated on her other side and asked, *"Kenst reden yiddish?"*

This gentleman simply shrugged that he too did not understand her. Just then, a well-dressed gentleman entered the train and stood in front of her. She looked up and asked, *"Kenst reden yiddish?"*

The man smiled and said, *"Ich farshtay yiddish..."* (I understand Yiddish).

The old woman gave a sigh and said, 'Oy, G-tt tzu danken (thank G-d)! *Zogt mir* (tell me), where do I get off to transfer to the D train?"

. . . .

A little old lady was flying on a plane to Israel. As the hostess passed the old woman, she was asked, "Could you please bring me a glass of water?"

The hostess brought her the water and left. A few minutes later, the little old woman rang the call button for the hostess, "Could you please bring me a glass of water?"

The hostess returned with the water and left. About ten minutes later, the little old lady rang the call button and again asked the hostess to please bring her a glass of water.

When the hostess returned with the water, she asked, "Do you feel ill?"

The little old lady smiled reassuringly, "No, but *oy*, am I thirsty!"

. . . .

A school teacher asked her students to write about their grandparents, and this is what they wrote:

Grandparents are a lady and a man who have no little children of their own. They like other people's.

Grandparents don't have to do anything except to be there when we come to see them. They are so old they shouldn't play hard or run. When they take us for a walk, they slow down past things like pretty leaves and caterpillars.

Grandparents don't say, "Hurry up."

When Grandparents read to us, they don't skip. They don't mind if we ask for the same story over and over again.

They let us have snacks before bedtime, and they say prayers with us every time, and kiss us even when we've acted bad.

. . . .

A very wealthy man had passed away. In the funeral chapel, a little old lady sat in one of the back rows sobbing uncontrollably.

As the service finished, the rabbi concluded by explaining that the last wish of the deceased was that his multi-million dollar fortune be equally distributed among his family. The services concluded and everyone left the chapel. But the little old lady remained behind and continued crying.

The funeral director, seeing this poor woman's hysteria, tried to comfort her. "You must have admired your uncle very much. He was a very generous man," he said.

The old woman continued sobbing and through tears exclaimed, "He wasn't my uncle..."

The funeral director corrected himself, "He must have been a very close relative to you," he continued.

The little old woman continued crying. "We weren't even related. I didn't even know him..."

The chapel director was puzzled. "Lady, if he wasn't a

relative and not even a friend, and you implied that you didn't even know this generous man who gave his fortune to his family, why are you crying."

The old lady sobbed, "That's why I'm crying!"

· ·

An elderly couple was sitting in a Senior Citizen center, watching a video. The old woman turned to her husband and asked, "Sam, could you please get me a glass of water?"

Her husband smiled and said, "Of course, my precious."

A few minutes later he came back with a glass of water and said, "Here you are, my dearest."

The old woman then turned to her husband and asked, "Sam, it's getting a little chilly in here. Could you please get me my sweater?"

Her husband smiled, "Of course, my darling."

A woman sitting next to the husband said softly, "You are a really amazing gentleman. I know you two have been married for over sixty years and I can't believe you still call your wife 'darling' and 'dear!'"

The old man smiled sheepishly, "I have to! I forgot her name!"

· ·

An elderly couple was spending a quiet evening together when the little old lady, in her 80's, turned to her husband and said, "David, I feel like a little ice cream with a little chocolate syrup on it." She repeated it a few times, then finally added, "Please go out and buy me some."

The old timer, David, got up from his chair to go out, when his wife stopped him, "Please, David, write it down. You'll forget what I want. Please, write it down."

The old man bristled, "Not necessary. I'll remember."

In a short while, he returned home with a little bag in which there was one bagel. The old lady sighed, "See, I told you, you'd forget! You forgot the cream cheese!"

. . . .

An elderly gentleman had serious hearing problems for a number of years. He went to the doctor who had him fitted for a set of hearing aids that allowed the gentleman to hear perfectly. The elderly gentleman went back in a month to the doctor and the doctor said, "Your hearing is perfect. Your family must be really pleased that you can hear again!"

The gentleman replied, "Oh, I haven't told my family yet. I just sit around and listen to the conversation. I've already changed my will three times!"

. . . .

An old timer lit up as he recognized a man walking in front of him down the subway stairs.

"Cohen!" he exclaimed. "I hardly recognized you. Why, you've gained at least thirty pounds since I saw you last, and

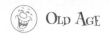

if I didn't see it myself, I'd swear you were at least two feet taller!"

The man looked at him and snapped, "I beg your pardon, but my name isn't Cohen."

"Aha!" laughed the first man, "So you even changed your name!"

. . . .

A n old timer was wishing his dear old friend a happy birthday and explained, "And I wish you should live to be 120 and 30 days."

The friend looked at him and, "Why the extra 30 days?"

The other old timer smiled and said, "When you go, I don't want you should go so suddenly!"

. . . .

C hana Kuchelman had struck it rich and decided to invite the fancy shmancy people in high society to her first big dinner. For the occasion, she hired a real English butler.

"Listen, Lancelot," she exclaimed, giving him final instructions. "My dentures don't fit too well. And sometimes when I talk, the upper set begins to slip down. Sometimes I don't realize it, but those who are watching me do. So I want you to watch me. If you see the teeth beginning to slip down, interrupt me with this code, 'Mr. Jones is at the door!' I'll understand and we won't have an accident."

The butler dutifully obliged and kept an eye on Mrs.

Kuchelman dentures all evening. When they began to slip, he said quietly, "Mr. Jones is at the door!"

Mrs. Kuchelman didn't hear him and continued to yak away at the dinner table. As the slipping dentures became more obvious, the butler called out sharply, *"Madam, I said Mr. Jones is at the door!"*

She kept talking and a few minutes later she noticed the butler trying to get her attention. "Excuse me, Lancelot, but did you say something?" she asked.

The butler sighed, with exasperation, "Yes Madam. I said Mr. Jones was at the door — but that was minutes ago — now he's in the chicken soup!"

. . . .

Finkelstein loved to play golf, but as the years were catching up on him, his eyesight started to fail. As a result, he kept losing ball after ball on the golf course.

One day, while discussing the problem with his friend, the friend suggested, "Listen, as a golfer, you're excellent, and if your eyes are bad, why don't you take Moscowitz along with you the next time you play golf? He has the eyes of an eagle and he'll be able to follow the ball perfectly."

Finkelstein looked at his friend and exclaimed, "Are you kidding me? Moscowitz is 93 years old!"

"That's true," exclaimed his friend, "But he has the sharp vision of an eagle."

So Finkelstein heeded his friend's advice. The next day when he went out to play, he picked up his friend Moscowitz

from the Metropolitan Jewish Geriatric Center and they went to the golf course.

"Now look," Finkelstein said to Moscowitz, as the old timer sat in his wheelchair at the first hole. "I'm going to hit the ball and you watch where it goes."

Finkelstein leaned over the ball, gave it a whack and the ball flew almost half a mile.

"Did you see it? Did you see it?" shouted Finkelstein.

"Did I see it?" replied Moscowitz, "Of course I saw it! Don't I have the eyes of an eagle?"

"Okay," shouted Finkelstein, "So tell me, where is it?"

Moscowitz, looking up at Finkelstein, a little embarrassed and sighed, "I forgot!"

. . . .

An old timer who was the pillar of strength in his community for years, began to develop insomnia and couldn't fall asleep at night. He tried everything — hot tea, a little Schnapps, warm cocoa, and all the home remedies his friends could suggest, but nothing worked.

Finally, as a last resort, his daughter took him to a doctor who examined the old timer and admitted he could not help. He suggested she take him to a psychiatrist who specialized in hypnotism.

The old timer went reluctantly, not knowing what to expect. When they got there, the psychiatrist told the daughter she could wait outside while he worked with her father alone.

"There's nothing to it," the psychiatrist explained. "All I will do is put him into a deep trance and, with the power of suggestion, your father's sleepless nights will be at an end."

The daughter was concerned. "Is it dangerous?" she asked.

"Of course not," the doctor explained. "Just wait in my outer office and when he goes under the trance I'll call you and you will see for yourself."

Once alone with the old man, he told him to lie down on the couch. "Now, you are resting. You will hear nothing but my voice. It will make you very sleepy. I can see that you are growing tired and you are getting very sleepy. Your eyes are getting heavy. You can hardly keep them open. Now your body is relaxed and every muscle is asleep. Now you are asleep...deep, deep asleep!"

The old timer lay still as the psychiatrist tiptoed out of the room to call in the daughter.

"You may go in now. And in a little while, I will wake him. From this moment on, his insomnia is at an end. You can take my professional opinion on that."

The young girl went inside and saw her father on the couch. "Pa — Papa can you hear me?" she whispered in his ear. "Are you really asleep at last?"

Very cautiously, the old man opened one fearful eye and asked softly, "Shirley, tell me — is the *meshugener* still here?"

Irving went to a psychiatrist and sat down for an interview. "Tell me," asked the psychiatrist, "Do you have trouble making up your mind?"

Irving thought for a moment then explained, "Well, yes and no."

"Tell me, what is the real reason you are having difficulty?" asked the psychiatrist.

"Well," explained Irving, "I have trouble remembering things."

"What kind of things?" asked the psychiatrist.

"Oh, just anything...dates, what I had for breakfast, where I left my laundry...you know." Irving explained.

"How long has this been going on?" asked the psychiatrist.

"How long has what been going on?" Irving asked.

· ·

It was during the dark days of the Depression when all the banks closed. Thousands lined up in front of the banks in the hope of getting at least some of their hard-earned savings salvaged. In front of one bank, there was a very long line, but right at the front of the line was a sweet old lady who stood quietly, while all the others were biting their nails, looks of anguish covering their faces.

A man standing next to the little old lady said softly, "You don't look the least bit disturbed. I guess you feel confident that the bank will open and you will get your money?"

The old lady smiled and said, "Who cares?"

"Lady," the man said, "You mean you're not even concerned about your money? Everyone here is concerned we might not even get a penny!"

The old lady sighed with a smile, "Who cares?"

"I don't understand you — how much do you have in this bank?" the man asked.

"I don't have any money in this bank," she replied.

"Then, for heaven's sake, what are you standing on line for?"

The old lady smiled meekly, "I'm waiting for the calendar!"

⸻

Malka had gotten her first paycheck in the mail while at grandma's house. "Bubby, please take the check to the bank next time you go and cash it for me."

When the old timer went to the bank, the teller said, "You'll have to endorse it."

The old lady was bewildered. "My daughter said to bring it to you. What do you mean 'endorse it'?"

The teller smiled and patiently explained, "Just sign the back, the same as you would in a letter."

The old lady took a pen and wrote on the back of the check, "So proud of you, Malka! Love, Bubby."

⸻

Show me a person with head held high and I'll show you a person who can't get used to bifocal glasses.

Two elderly ladies, who could barely see over the car's dashboard, went through a red light at an intersection. One of them rubbed her eyes, didn't say a word, and thought to herself, "I think I'm either seeing things or I'm getting color blind. I could have sworn that was a red light we just went through!"

As they rode along, they crossed another intersection and again they went through a red light.

"I'm sure that light was red, but I guess I was wrong," she thought to herself once more.

When they hit another intersection and another red light, once more the car went through. One of the ladies called to her companion. "Mildred, you know, we just ran through three red lights. You could have killed us!"

Mildred turned to her friend and exclaimed, "Oh, am I driving?"

· ·

Two very elderly ladies were enjoying the sunshine on a park bench in Miami. They had been meeting at that park every day for over twelve years, just making idle chatter and enjoying their friendship.

One day, the younger of the two turned to the other and said, "Please don't be angry with me, my dear, but I am embarrassed after all these years, what is your name? I'm trying to remember but I just can't."

The older friend stared at her, looking very distressed, said nothing for two full minutes, then finally asked, "How soon do you have to know?"

· ·

When Mama and Papa celebrated their 50th wedding anniversary last month, Papa wanted to get Mama a huge bouquet of flowers. So he asked her, "Tell me, what's your favorite flower?"

Mama, quite taken aback, cooed "After all these years and you still don't know? It's Pillsbury!"

· ·

While waiting for my first appointment in the reception room of a new dentist, I noticed his certificate, which bore his full name. Suddenly, I remembered that a boy with the same name had been in preschool with me some fifty years ago. Upon seeing him, however, I quickly discarded such a thought. The balding, gray-haired man with the deeply lined face was way too old to have been my classmate.

After he had examined my teeth, I asked him if he had attended the same preschool as I did.

"Yes," he replied.

"You were in my class!" I exclaimed.

He looked at me closely, and then asked, "What did you teach?"

Relationships

A young man was having difficulty getting along with his wife and went to his rabbi for help. The rabbi listened intently and then said, "I suggest you run five miles each day for a week. The fresh air in your lungs might help calm you down. Call me next week to let me know how it's working out for both of you."

The following week, the rabbi got a call from the young man. "Hello rabbi, remember you asked me to call you back?"

"Good. So tell me, how are things working out for you?" the rabbi asked.

The young man declared, "Great! I'm thirty-five miles from home. What should I do now?"

A little old lady met her neighbor and exclaimed, "I just can't stand that woman who moved in next door to me!"

Her friend smiled, "What's so terrible about her?"

"Terrible," replied the little old lady. "A whole day long she says terrible things about her husband. All she does is complain. No one man could be that bad! Now, take me for example. My husband drinks like a fish, he gambles every minute he's away from the house, he stays out late, a worse *trombenik* (loafer) you never saw. But do you ever hear me say a word to anybody?"

. . . .

A father was talking to his son, who was planning to get married. "Sheldon, my boy, Mama and I have been married for 45 years. When we got married, we agreed that I would take care of all the major problems that might come up, and she would take of all the minor ones."

"That's wonderful!" the son exclaimed. "Does it really work?"

"It works perfectly, because to date, no large problems have ever come up."

"But what if you have a difference of opinion?" the boy asked.

"If we have a difference of opinion and Mama happens to be right, I accept her opinion."

"But what if you happen to be right?" the son asked.

The father smiled and replied, "Oh, to tell you the truth, that has never happened."

• •

A rabbi was once asked by a group of teenagers to define marriage. The old timer thought for a moment, then declared, "A good marriage is like a violin being played. When the music is over the strings are still attached."

• •

A woman applying for a loan at a local bank was asked, "What's your husband's average home income?"

The woman replied, "About one o'clock in the morning, why?"

• •

A young lady goes to a *shadchan* (matchmaker) and says she is looking for a husband. "You see, the man I want must be an outstanding personality, know the latest news and gossip, be able to tell jokes, and sing and dance. He must neither drink nor smoke, always be on call, yet be quiet when I need peace of mind."

The matchmaker sighed, "Lady, you're not looking for a husband, you're looking for a television. Come to me when you're ready to marry a real person!"

A young man who was about to get married asked his friends who had been married for close to fifty years, "How come you and your wife have gotten along so well for all these years?"

The old timer smiled and said, "It's very simple. We never have any arguments. In the morning, she does exactly what she wants, and in the afternoon, I do exactly what she wants!"

. . . .

An elderly couple has dinner at another couple's house and after eating, the wives leave the table and go into the kitchen.

The two elderly gentlemen are talking, and one says, "Last night we went out to a new restaurant and it was really great. I would recommend it very highly."

The other man says, "What's the name of the restaurant?"

The first man knits his brow in obvious concentration and finally says, "Uh, what is the name of that red flower you give to people on special occasions?"

His friend replies, "A carnation?"

"No, no. The other one. You know, the one that is red and has thorns?"

His friend says, "Do you mean a rose?"

"Yes, yes that's it! Thank you!" the first man says.

He then turns toward the kitchen and calls out, "Rose, what's the name of that restaurant we went to last night?"

An old-timer was talking to his attorney as he prepared his will. "I have only one living relative, a nephew," the old-timer explained to his lawyer. "But the kid is a pain in the neck, a no-*goodnik* of the first order. I don't want to leave him anything."

"You can't do that," explained the lawyer. "You must recognize your blood relatives in your will or the whole will would be contested in the courts."

The old-timer listened and wrote out his will. It was duly filed in his attorney's safe and a few years later, the old-timer passed away.

When it came time to read the will, the attorney notified everyone whose name appeared in the will. They came to the reading of the last will and testament of the dearly departed Abraham Foofnik.

"To my dear friend, Mendel Schwartz, I leave $5,000 for the wonderful things he has done for people. To my butcher, Chaim Goldberg, who gave me the finest cuts of meat during all the shortages, I leave $5,000. To my superintendent, who always came up when I had to have something in the house fixed, I leave $6,000. And to my blood relative, Stanley Foofnik, of whom I want to recognize in my will, 'Hello Stanley!'"

· ·

As the newly elected president of his shul, Goldberg got up to address the congregation. He began, "Ladies and gentlemen, I'm a man of few words..."

A fellow sitting in the first row sighed, "Yeh, yeh, I'm also married."

. . . .

Cohen met his friend on the street. "What's new?" the friend asked.

"My wife lost her credit card last week," Cohen replied.

"Did you report it missing yet?" the friend asked.

"Of course not!" Cohen exclaimed.

"Why?" the friend asked.

"Why not?" Cohen replied, "Because the party who found it has been spending less than she did!"

. . . .

Cohen's son-in-law came into his office and said, "Hey Pop, could you loan me $200, please?" Cohen did not answer.

The youth continued, "Hey Pop, could you loan me $200?" Cohen did not answer.

The youth was growing angry and shouted, "Why don't you answer me?"

The old man sighed and replied, "Isn't it better I should owe you an answer than you should owe me the $200?"

Hymie was talking to a friend, "I have a mother-in-law who's just impossible! Whatever I get her for a Chanukah present, she exchanges. If I get her a black pocketbook, she exchanges it for a brown one. If I get her a fancy Shabbos robe, she complains it is too big or too small and exchanges it for something else. So this year, I outsmarted her and I gave her a $20 gift certificate."

"*Nu*, so what happened?" his friend asked.

"She exchanged it for two $10 certificates!"

. . . .

It was some Bar Mitzvah. The room was filled with flowers, ice statues shaped as swans spouting colored punch adorned the tables. The Mermelsteins arrived and were taken aback by the ostentatiousness of the affair.

Spotting the Mermelsteins, Mrs. Spielberg, the hostess, walked over and, with a great flourish gasped, "Darlings, you came to my Simcha! I'm so happy! Isn't this some affair?" she asked, seeking a favorable response.

"Oh, yes," they replied. "Beautiful, simply beautiful! And where's the Bar Mitzvah boy?"

"He's with his friends. But come, first I want to show you the beautiful statue of my Herbert; it's made from chopped liver, you know. Look at the exquisite detail!" she beamed.

The Mermelsteins could not control themselves, and in true cultured fashion, quipped, "We've never seen anything the equal of it. Who made it — Jaques Lipshitz or Epstein?"

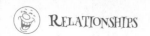

Mrs. Spielberg smiled warmly and exclaimed, "Lipshitz of course. You know, Epstein only works in Halavah."

. . . .

Joe asked Yankel, "Yankel, I haven't seen you in three weeks. What's new with you?"

"Well," replied Yankel, "Three weeks ago my favorite aunt died. She was a sweet, lovable, generous person and she left me $25,000. Last week, would you believe it, my favorite uncle passed away — a warm, smiling prince of a man. I shall truly miss him. He also left me money — $50,000. This week, however, nothing!"

. . . .

One cannibal said to the other, "You know something, Irving? I really don't like my mechanic."

The other answered, "So, just eat the vegetables."

. . . .

Sadie came home one night with a very fancy hat box. She exclaimed to her husband, "Sam, I want you should look at the beautiful creation I purchased today." She opened the box and took out a hat that was a sheer monstrosity. "Look at this hat, isn't it beautiful? And it only cost $150!"

"What? $150 for that monstrosity? That's a sin with children starving all over the world today."

Sadie stiffened up, put the hat on and then snapped, "*Nu* so the sin is on my head!"

. . . .

Sadie, a new mother-in-law, cried to her friend, "*Oy*, a curse has befallen me! My daughter married a young man and we are cursed because he does not know how to drink, nor does he know how to gamble."

"He doesn't know how to drink and he doesn't know how to gamble," exclaimed the friend, "That, you consider a curse? My friend, that is a blessing."

"No, no!" sighed the old woman, "You see, he doesn't know how to drink and he *drinks*, and he doesn't know how to gamble, yet he *gambles!*"

. . . .

Sadie walked into her butcher store one day with a beautiful diamond ring on her finger.

"Something new?" asked the butcher.

"Yeah, my mother-in-law gave it to me before she passed away," Sadie explained.

"How come?" asked the butcher. "You always said the two of you didn't get along and that she never gave you any gifts. So how come such a gift?"

Well," Sadie began, "Before she passed away, she gave me $3,000 and said I should buy a stone after she passed away — so I did!"

adie was reading a newspaper as Sam was resting nearby. "Sam," she exclaimed, "It says here that in India, a man doesn't know his wife until he marries her."

Sam yawned and exclaimed, "And isn't it the same here?"

. . . .

am was talking with a friend, "Oy, does Louie have a wife. She can talk for any hours on any subject."

His friend sighed, "Mine doesn't need a subject!"

. . . .

arah Clugsmutter went to a marriage counselor and told her the problem she had. The marriage counselor sympathized with her and said, "Maybe your problem is that you've been waking up grumpy in the morning."

The woman sighed, "I do not. I always let him sleep."

. . . .

arah woke her husband Irving in the middle of the night. "Irving, wake up quick, I think there's a mouse in the room — I can hear it squeaking!"

Irving, awoken from a sound sleep, snapped, "Nu, so what do you want me to do? Oil it?"

Two fathers were talking. "*Nu,* so what did you get for Father's Day?" The other old timer replied, "The bills from Mother's Day."

. . . .

Two Garment Center jobbers met on the street. "Hello Sam," Abe exclaimed. "I understand you have a very fancy mother-in-law."

"What do you mean 'fancy?'" Sam questioned soulfully.

"Well, I heard she's now attending Columbia University!"

"*Nu?*" sighed Sam.

"*Nu?* Are you kidding? A woman her age going to a university like Columbia? That's wonderful! Tell me, what is she studying?" Abe questioned.

Sam sighed once more and replied, "She's not studying anything — they're studying her!"

. . . .

Two men were discussing the attributes of their respective mothers-in-law. "Let me tell you something," the first man began. "I went with mine to the racetrack last week and even though it was her first time, she won four races!"

"Amazing!" countered the second man. "Mine gets winded just walking up the steps to our house!"

Little Gems

friend of mine just told me the phone company even has a telephone number for atheists.

It's the same number as Dial-a-Prayer — only nobody answers.

pessimist was asked, "What is the difference between an optimist and a pessimist?"

To which he replied, "A pessimist says, 'We've hit the lowest point, the situation can't get any worse.' An optimist says, 'No, it can still get worse!'"

A word to today's generation: The only time success comes before work is in the dictionary.

. . . .

Based on the overwhelming spending going on in Washington these days, isn't it true that an elephant is a mouse built to government specifications?

. . . .

I've always wondered how come generous people seldom have emotional and mental problems?

. . . .

I finally figured out what a filing cabinet is to be used for. It's a place where you lose things alphabetically.

. . . .

I've always wondered how a lawyer can write a document of 5,000 words and call it a brief!

. . . .

Isn't it so true…when a man answers a telephone, he reaches for a pencil. When a woman answers the phone, she reaches for a chair!

Life is really a vicious cycle. Some people lose their health getting wealthy. And then lose their wealth getting healthy.

. . . .

Money — It can buy a house, but not a home. It can buy a clock, but not time. It can buy you a position, but not respect. It can buy you a bed, but not sleep. It can buy you a book, but not knowledge. It can buy you medicine, but not health. It can buy you blood, but not life.

. . . .

Revolving credit plan: Every time you turn around you have to make a payment.

. . . .

Question: What business is a *Yenta* in?

Answer: Yours!

. . . .

The world is filled with three types of people: The *Schlemiels*, the *Schlemazels* and the *Nudniks*.

The *Schlemiel* is clumsy; he always spills his soup. And where does the soup fall? On the *Schlemazel's* pants of course!

And where is the *Nudnik* in all this? He wants to know what kind of soup it was — chicken, noodle, or vegetable.

. . . .

To err is human. To blame it on someone else is politics.

. . . .

When two men are in a business and always agree, one of them is unnecessary.

. . . .

Who was it who told me a wrench is a Jewish resort with horses?

. . . .

You got to smile! A smile costs nothing, but gives so much. It enriches those who receive it without making poorer those who give. It takes but a moment, but the memory of it sometimes lasts forever.

None is so rich or mighty that he could get along without it, and none is so poor that he can't be made rich by it.

A smile creates happiness in the home, fosters good will in business, and is the sign of friendship.

It brings rest to the weary, cheer to the discouraged, sunshine to the sad and it is nature's best antidote for trouble.

Yet it cannot be bought, begged, borrowed or stolen, for it is something that is of no value to anyone until it is given away.

Some people are too tired to give you a smile. Give them one of yours — as none needs a smile so much as he who has no more to give.

Classic Jewish Tales
— Collector's Edition —

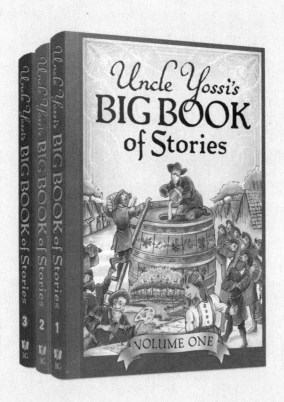

Over **60** classic Jewish stories drawn
from the Midrash, Talmud, and Jewish lore.
Instilling a love of G-d, love of the Torah,
and love of the Jewish people.

www.GreatJewishTales.com